AF553769

WOMEN EMPOWERMENT AND EDUCATION

WOMEN EMPOWERMENT AND EDUCATION

Edited by

Dr. S.K. Panneer Selvam

Assistant Professor

Dept. of Education

Bharathidasan University

Tamil Nadu

(India)

DISCOVERY PUBLISHING HOUSE PVT. LTD.

NEW DELHI-110 002

Published by:
Tilak Wasan

DISCOVERY PUBLISHING HOUSE PVT. LTD.
4383/4B, Ansari Road, Darya Ganj
New Delhi-110 002 (India)
Phone : +91-11-23279245, 43596064-65
Fax : +91-11-23253475
E-mail : parul.wasan@gmail.com
discoverypublishinghouse@gmail.com
web : www.discoverypublishinggroup.com

***First Edition:* 2013**

ISBN: 978-93-5056-310-6

Women Empowerment and Education

Printed at:
Dynamic Printers
Delhi

Preface

Humanists have defined the 'culture' in many ways. The British Humanist, Sir Edward Burnett Tylor, who lived in the end of 19th century defined 'culture' in the following words. "It is the life style with Knowledge, Belief, Arts, Law, Conduct, Tradition and other conventions. Habits and customs promoted through the relationship of male and female to be attained by mankind." An analysis of the combined activities of men and women with the definition as 'Culture' would bring out the truth that it has two different norms for male and female. Kate Millet, in this regard says, "We fail to note that in the social hierarchy male ruling over the female has been made as a birth right and they refrain from accepting. Through this set up a seasoned internal colonization's obtained. The reason for this trend may be that our society remaining simians Pastiarchalcial society. Before this trend started to gain its momentum it was matriarchal society stood well." So, it is necessary to explain the rise and fall of matriarchal society. Liberation is born from the Latin word "Liber", meaning drawing independence from social and political dominance. Feminists speak of liberation of women. When rights are common, it is kept in mind that woman should get equal rights in education and job opportunities. Liberation, in this context, refers to freedom for woman from suppression in the family, social and industrial concerns. Total freedom is not obtained even in industrially and educationally advanced countries. But this aim and object of Liberation of woman cannot be viewed in its narrow sense. Still, India far lacking behind in this regard, compared with other countries, in the name of religion, culture and customs. However, the truth brings out a different picture in the case of India and its neighboring countries, Pakistan, Bangladesh, Sri Lanka and Burma. The reign of woman have been witnessed in the past and present. But, it was the individual woman who stood against all the ads and came to power setting example to the woman tolk take the lead-role. Women can be empowered only by educating and imparting skills. Education and skills will certainly make them self reliant and resourceful wherever and whenever they come across problems. They must fully enjoy bargaining power, influencing power, and decision making power access to resources and have experience of economic and political world. A revolving fund helps the members draw from it for medical and education expenses or to meet out marriage commitments and undertake family obligations. Sometimes members turn to it to support their husband's business enterprises. It has inculcated the habit of saving and also provided them with a sense of security. Leadership qualities developed through SHG meetings have seen 2500 women become presidents or members of panchayats and local bodies in Tamilnadu. Education as such, results in positive externalities. Not only does it have an intrinsic value in the sense of the joy of learning, reading etc, but it also has instrumental, social and process roles. Moreover education may spread through interpersonal motivation. When one individual sends her child to school, her neighbour is likely to do so as well. Women's education too, often spreads this way, more specifically, through same sex effects. I.e. an educated woman is far more likely to send her daughter to school than an uneducated woman. Also, she is likely to maintain better conditions of nutrition and hygiene in her household and thereby improve her family's health (Sen 1997). The presence of a larger number of female teachers may encourage parents to send their daughters to school. Thus education is a fundamental tool for women's empowerment. The originality of this edition owes to the contributors. As an editor I acknowledged to the contributors.

—Author

Contents

CHAPTER

1

Education to Women and the Fundamental Right of Empowerment

Introduction

The best creation of God on the Earth is man and women. The selective memento presented to man and woman by the creator is equal rights to both. The rights were rightly exercised in this soil. The heroine of *Ramayana*; an epic this ancient soil respects much gave the right of choosing her companion through *Swayamwara*. The Emperor *Dasarada* gave due respect to his wife *Kaikeye* and honoured his promises knowing fully he will lose himself. It was Bharatha who refused even his mother's wish of becoming the ruler of *Ayothi*. This epic depicts the patent style of life of the people giving due rights and privileges to women and respecting each other even during turmoil's. It was *Rama* denied permission to Site to accompany him to *Vanavasa*. *Lakshman*, a loyal and Seeta brother of Rama extended security and safety to his sister-in-law Seeta for fourteen years, sleepless, during Vanavasa.

The life style without disparity by sex was the order of the society thousands of years ago. Even *Sangam* periods in South did not leave evidence for the prevalence of discrimination by sex. And women were playing leading role as with case of men and it could be understood from the fact that fifteen out of fifty poets who composed poems were women and there were no historical evidence for the sexual discrimination. Women were able to venture out and played an equal role in and out of the house.

History and Women

Up to 18th century the society did not see women as a different one and there are no historical and classical evidences to sex descriptions and to more extent women were considered to be more respectable part of the life. In every success of a man there was a woman behind him. Men respected, loved and admired women with much regard, and it is a man, named. *ShahJahan,* who loved even after the death of *Mumtaj* and built a monument, stands still a marvel of the world. But a thorough study to find the period, situation and reasons for the discrimination between man and woman is needed to find the origin of this pevennial problem. In any society, developed or developing the role of the woman and contribution from them cannot be undermined. Though man is created as it is whether directly or indirectly considerable with certain special features, women also have some uniqueness equally. In every action of man woman is vied to place at the receiving end.

We need to think the striking feature of the woman of the twentieth and twenty first century has the intelligence and accumulated knowledge thanks to the reformations and renaissance took place everywhere by the efforts of leaders who took much strain and pain for the independence of women from the clutches of biased society. "Nearly 450 million adult women in developing countries are stunted as a result of childhood protein energy malnutrition".

Industrial Revolution an Eye-Opener

The Industrial Revolution in England during 18th century had brought in many changes in the attitudes of the society. The theory and system of Division of Labour took the place of Division of work between men and women. India which never had a common political and cultural uniformity and conformity till the arrival of British each region and religion had its own way of treating the women. The entry and the rule of law by the British made the people of Bharath to unite together in the name of freedom struggle and already history has registered the names of Women Rulers, *Chittaur Rani, Padmini, Ranimangamma* and later *Anne Beasant, Sarojini Naidu* and *Vijayalakshmi Pandit,* as freedom fighters the society did not prevent the women from playing active role in politics.

Till the end of 18th century, women in India enjoyed as protective assets and the natural barrier imposed upon the women had denied them certain privileges, like educational, cultural, professional opportunities enjoyed by the men. The Industrial Revolution spread in Europe and America has introduced three types of Feminism.

1. Liberal Feminism
2. Socialist Feminism
3. Radical Feminism.

Liberal Feminism

An approach to feminism was to be mooted after the Industrial Revolution took place and at the end of the 18th century Liberal Feminism came into existence. Marywollston Craft in her book 'A vindication of the Rights of women' had formulated this Feminism and the advocated for women the equal rights with men and the contemporary writer and social reformer John Stuart Mill in his book titled 'Subjection of women' had emphasized that the women should be permitted to have the rights to choose her own way of life and law should render equality to women and he stressed the need for the women to get voting right, right in the property and choosing a career to maintain her own dignity.

There were another set of writers who were also of the opinion that of women (or) female to have an identity of their own, at the beginning, had started to slide and advised the woman folk not to leave the family set up. Hence, they were branded as moderates. Gradually the Liberal Feminism started to bring reforms with social and family life of women.

Socialist Feminism

This could be considered as a child of Marxism. This Feminism stood against the women's code of life of family, property and bearing and rearing child. Socialist feminism found its root from the philosophy of Fredrik Angels and Karl Marx who thought for the total independence of entire humanity, from the clutches of anarchism, especially the working class. The active and productive role permitted during pre-historic period had been denied to women in the Agricultural Society. Under this system the female was brought under the male. The women were suppressed in all walks of life. And modern capitalism was relentless towards this approach. Her household activities were not valued in terms of money and it was taken as service to her family and like communal discrimination, sexual discrimination got rooted deeply. The women sect was treated as a mammoth cheaper labour force.

Radical Feminism

Radical Feminism gave its birth to break socio-family system wherein women were controlled on sexual basis. The forerunners of Radical Feminism preferred to break the paternal domination, as the biological differences were the basis of that.

Radical Feminists hated male for their churlish domination over female. They advocated the strong feeling of total independence of women from male. It enabled one to understand that the female is superior to man. Radical Feminism welcomes the feminine leadership. This 'ism' included aspects of Matriarchal Society. The women were considered fully qualified in production as she plays a predominant role in the division of work in the reproduction.

A deep insight into the three kinds of feminism would enable one to understand the principles of feminism. The classics of contemporary literature have given an account on feminism and the scenes were different from place to place and time to time. Though contribution of female domestically and the gross value of the volume of work is remarkable the role could be played externally were curbed in the name of religion customs and culture.

The Concepts of Feminism

The feminist stalwarts have classified the concepts to understand the Socio-Economic conditions of the females who were suppressed mentally.

They are,

1. Structure of culture
2. Matriarchal society
3. Patriarchal society
4. Sexual division of labour
5. Sexual politics
6. Power
7. Liberation.

Though the concepts of feminism formulated in the foreign countries, one should not conclude that it is confined to the cultural background of those countries only. It has global character to understand the slavery of women; still, it should be understood from the common cultural background.

The Structure of Culture

Humanists have defined the 'culture' in many ways. The British Humanist, Sir Edward Burnett Tylor, who lived in the end of 19th century defined 'culture' in the following words. "It is the life style with Knowledge, Belief, Arts, Law, Conduct, Tradition and other conventions. Habits and customs promoted through the relationship of male and female to be attained by mankind."

An analysis of the combined activities of men and women with the definition as 'Culture' would bring out the truth that it has two different norms for male and female. Kate Millet, in this regard says, "We fail to note that in the social hierarchy male ruling over the female has been made as a birth right and they refrain from accepting. Through this set up a seasoned internal colonization's obtained. The reason for this trend may be that our society remaining simians Pastiarchalcial society. Before this trend started to gain its momentum it was matriarchal society stood well." So, it is necessary to explain the rise and fall of matriarchal society.

Matriarchal Society

In this society, female were given importance and they enjoyed supreme status. It could be learnt that in the evolution of mankind, woman was the backbone and she played a key role in all constructive processes.

Under this matrilineal society:

1. Woman was not depending upon the man.
2. Maternal relatives were respected much.
3. The hereditary of a person was studied from the character of mother.
4. The children were under the guard of the mother while the father was hunting.
5. The belief on god was on motherly basis only.

Patriarchal Society

According to Sociologists and Feminists "Patriarchal society got stabilized through the relationship between the right of individual ownership and subordinate status of woman".

The patriarchal society came into existence with two meanings.

1. Rule of men
2. Rule of father.

In the words of Rubin and Angels, "The patriarchs imbibe male's domination within itself and rule the woman, youngster, child and slave and maid servant and suppress them." However, the feminists agree his point that female domination was prevalent in the patriarchal society. The Capitalistic Pattern of society, individual's right on property and subordination made the woman, who was enjoying equal rights, independence and the factor of production of life and productive forces in the society, to become dependents and subordinates and Einstein also agreed with this view.

Simone de Beanvoir replies, "Man considers that woman is different from him and he states that woman is not permitted to have her own identity and treated as model of man and men plays the role of subject and the women is permitted to be objects".

Sexual Division of Labour

Ann Oakley accepts the view that it is natural that woman performing domestic duties, it is necessary and global. To explain this he submits three points. They are,

1. Biologically man going for hunting, woman remaining in the house.
2. Under the Humanitarian ground man is always stronger and woman becomes weaker while conceiving and rearing the child. The sex myth is the cause for the man and woman differently themselves. It reproduced the social set up and made impact on all societies.
3. Sociologists claim that division of work is pertaining to sex and it is necessary for the home.

So, division of work sexually is based on sex discrimination.

Sex and Gender

Sex is biological. It consists of man and woman. In the discrimination woman plays a supportive role and woman is made a companion of man. A man loving a woman is welcomed. Feminity is considered holy and sublime. Woman is considered as reproducing plant. Her individuality is not allowed to exist. She is made to remain as a subordinate to man. In Gender discrimination it is taught that this work done is different naturally and its value also differs. It points out that the woman is confined to child learning and rearing only and both of them kept under the control of man.

According to German Feminist Maria Mies, "Woman is connected with nature. The nature and the woman does identical job of production. But both do not try to exert influence or domination over anything. The body of the woman is made not to belong to her and likewise to the earth. Particularly the body of the woman and the nature produce the society and history."

Sexual Politics

Sexual politics, according to active feminist Gate Millet, means the Power System of relationship of man and woman. The sexual relations and its internal power roots into the family system. So, the family has given primary place to man and secondary place to woman.

The sexual politics is implemented through temperament, role and status. Knowledge, Aggression, Strength and Skill has become prerequisites of man and Politeness, Humbleness, Illiteracy, Chastity, Dependability and Inability have been made symbol of feminist. Woman drowned by sexual politics tries to identify and recognize herself within man. In the economic front also woman is pushed back and even after acquiring educational and academic qualifications and qualities they are placed at the rear seat. H.R. Hays also regrets that because of biological differences woman is treated inferior and all the concepts related and pertaining to woman are designed by man and the model of woman is also created by man.

The psychology, pusillanimous role, social status of woman are built as marital and family relationship and the liberty of sex of woman is made politics and the politics means the domination of man. Sexual politics gives powers and rights to man.

Power

The power exercised in sexual politics defines the freedom of man. The politics absorbs the Gender and this type of power, "Makes the social status of woman an unequal. It places the woman at the secondary level in politics and culture". It ceases the opportunities of acquiring resources for the life and an imbalance prevails in rights and duties. The industrial market and educational training is pushed towards man and woman is treated 'others' and her movements are curtailed on the basis of biological factors and weaknesses, mentally and physically.

When the power is exercised, it leads to violence on woman and as it comes out of patriarchal relations, it is made social practices of the society. Whenever inequality prevails, violence erupts. Power gets stimulated with relations between sex and violence. So, it could be presumed that violence is an outcome of male domination.

Liberation

Liberation is born from the Latin word "Liber", meaning drawing independence from social and political dominance. Feminists speak of liberation of women. When rights are common, it is kept in mind that woman should get equal rights in education and job opportunities. Liberation, in this context, refers to freedom for woman from suppression in the family, social and industrial concerns. Total freedom is not obtained even in industrially and educationally advanced countries. But this aim and object of Liberation of woman cannot be viewed in its narrow sense. Still, India far lacking behind in this regard, compared with other countries, in the name of religion, culture and customs. However, the truth brings out a different picture in the case of India and its neighbouring countries, Pakistan, Bangladesh, Sri Lanka and Burma. The reign of woman have been witnessed in the past and present. But, it was the individual woman who stood against all the ads and came to power setting example to the woman talk take the lead-role.

Status of Women in the Present Era

Status of women refers to the position as individuals in the social structure defined by their designated rights and obligations. The concept of status sociologically implies hierarchical arrangement of social positions with the access to and control over material resources, including food, and income and to social resources including knowledge power and prestige within the family, community and society at large. The status and problems of *dalit* woman and children, of working women, of house wives, of tribal woman, of Muslim woman, or of lettered and unlettered rural women are all related to gender cult and issues related to shall be addressed after thorough and careful studies. In the hierarchy of problems domestic violence in one form or the other, and struggle between 'haves' and 'have-nots' are the perennial ones and the education to women could be the best medicine to cure.

Women's studies began in U.S.A. in late sixties itself whereas in India after the International Women's Year in 1975 and it is hoped that these studies can change. Women's lives and mobilize women to change their position and it can change the society and its values. The dimensions of development that need to be focused. While the academic development is the main thrust it is widely recognized that initiatives and provisions need to be made for the developments of other dimensions also.

(a) Physical development: This would include providing relevant sex education, awareness about reproduction, knowledge on health and nutrition.

(b) Intellectual development: This includes ability to think critically, take independent decisions so that they become self-reliant.

(c) Emotional development: This would include skills to handle the various stresses and conflicts that women are subjected to at homes, in the society and at work place.

(d) Social development: The skills in handling inter-personal relations and ability to communicate to assertive and uphold their legal and other rights.

(e) Vocational development: Women need vocational information and guidance's about the wide choice available in the job market.

(f) Moral and spiritual development: Women have to be helped with value classifications to provide them the strength required to maintain a balanced view of life.

(g) Cultural development: Women do have a key role to play in maintaining and promoting the rich cultural heritage of the nation even in the modernization process.

Education to Women as a Ladder to Empowerment

The problems that need our attention while giving a thought to women's education in particular and the situations in general are manifold and complex in nature. Women constitute 48 per cent of the human resources and potential work force in India, psychologists and sociologists are quite sure that general ability among women is the same as men.

And there is an increasing realization among the states-men and Humanists that if a nation is to progress in various dimensions, then, women should be educated to participate in a much larger variety of walks of life than what are open for them at present. Education Commissions (RadhaKrishnan Commission) 1948, Kothari Commission (1967) suggests measures on women in the following words. "That role of women outside the home has become an important feature of the social and economic life of the country". And further suggests they should have free access to courses in arts, humanities, science and technology, courses in home science, nursing, education and social work need to be developed as these have attraction for a larger proportion of girls and facilities for advanced training in business administration and management should also be provided. History of formal education and role of various organisations in the promotion of literacy and education of women.

English rule in India, when political, legal and social institutions came to be established in the territory directly governed by the East India Company, can be set said to start about 1772 Literacy and education in this early period was intimately linked with a proselytizing work of the missionaries. By end of 1850, the number of schools had risen to 354 with 11,500 girls on the rolls. There were 99 boarding schools with 2400 girls attending them.

By the turn of the 20th century, all over India, there were 12 colleges, 467 secondary schools and 5,628 primary schools for girls with a total enrollment of 4,444,470 students. The First Five Year Plan (1951-56) advocated the need for adopting special measures to solve the problems of women's education. It recommended that the secondary as well as the university level, there should be a vocational approach so that those who complete such stages may at once take some vocation.

The Second Five Year Plan (1956-61) continued with the need for overall expansion of educational facilities. In 1959 a National Commission on Women Education was formed and its report had considerable influence on the framing of the Third Five Year Plan. It recommended condensed school courses for adult woman, the training of Bala Sevikas and Child Care programmes. This trend continued in the Fourth (1974-78) Plan. The Sixth Plan (1980-85) was an important landmark because for the first time a special chapter was devoted to women's development. Two documents of far reaching effect were the Report of the Committee on the Status of Women (CSW) and the National Perspective Plan for Women (NPPW). Since then many programmes and schemes were launched which had direct or indirect bearing on women's education: They are,

1. Assistance for Voluntary Agencies for Rural Development (AVARD),
2. Council for Advancement of People's Action for Rural Technology (CAPART),
3. District Institute for Education and Training (DIET),
4. District Rural Development Agency (DRDA),
5. Functional Literacy for Adult Women (FLAW),
6. Integrated Rural Development Programme (IRDP), and
7. Women's Integrated Learning for Life. (WILL).

Irrespective of many active programmes and schemes, the Literacy percentage still low as,

In 1951 total - 18.33 per cent women - 8.86 per cent

1991 total - 52.11 per cent women - 39.25 per cent

2001 total - 65.38 per cent women - 54.16 per cent.

One is forced to presume that women's education will never reach great heights unless the males are not 'educated' to look at women's education with interest and give to it their unstinted support. *In spite* of all these hurdles, the figures related to Literacy rate in India, in 2001, in rural,

46.70 and in urban, 73.20 female have been getting education and it may give some consolation for the advocates of women's education and development.

Position of Women in Higher Education

Looking on the data available from 300 universities in India, there are 11 women Vice Chancellors, one Pro-Vice Chancellor, 3 Women Registrars, 66 Women Deans, 13 Women Directors, 12 Women Librarians. But comparing to other countries the women's representation in Assemblies and Parliament is much higher.

Bottlenecks in Achieving Leadership Position

Whatever the arguments put forth towards women's education for their empowerment in the society there are still some bottlenecks and it is left with the individual parent-family and the female child concerned to make herself an able woman to resist and come over all the hurdles come in her way throughout her career internally and externally.

Some of the bottlenecks, women in general and come across are:

- Sexist and sex-role attitudes towards women's ability to lead or perform administrative and managerial functions.
- Traditional mindset of roles, food habit and life style has not changed. This adds to the family responsibility. The dual role of performing unpaid work at home, rearing and tutoring children and working in the work place.
- Lack of traditional mentoring opportunities for women.
- Lack of access to socialization process, which limit women from aspiring to leadership position.
- Higher positions demand longer hours of working, lot of long as well as short distance travel and attending late meetings.

- Dinner diplomacy and late night get together forbid her from organizing/participating in the culture of educational organizations.
- Women, whatever may be the level of the position held, are afraid of character assassination.

Suggestions

It is accepted universally that education liberates women from ignorance and enhances her self-esteem. It enables them to choose their own way and look after their families in a better way. It is the appropriate place to quote, Napoleon Bonaparte's words, "Give me an educated mother, I shall promise the birth of a civilized nation". So, in the present context, the following suggestions could be submitted. The problem of gender discrimination needs to be dealt with on several fronts.

- On the economic front, to reduce inequalities and to strike for social justice it is suggested that the amount of Labour done by the housewives must be calculated and added to the Gross Domestic Product.
- The amount of Labour done by house wife is never taken in for calculation in terms of money.
- On the legal front, not only to enact legislation aimed at social and sexual equality but also to devise means for their implementation.
- On the cultural front, to recognize, the rich qualities of women and also create an understanding among the various sections of the society.
- On the social front, to mobilize not only opinion but also purposeful action, and in the educational front, to unstill and understanding of dangers of gender discrimination among all persons living in every nook and corner of the society.

REFERENCES

1. Anuradha Mathu, Women's Studies Centers and the Status of Women, *University News*, 40(49), Dec. 9 -15, 2002.
2. Archana Tomer & Sneha Joshi, Initiative for Women Managers in Higher Education, *University News*, 41(09), March 03-09, 2003.
3. Gowri Srivastava, Growth in the Higher Education of Women in India, *University News*. (40/11), March 17-23, 2003.
4. Indiresan.J, (2002), Education for Women's Empowerment: *Gender—Positive Initiatives in Pace-Setting Women's College*, Konark Publishers, New Delhi.
5. Indiresan, J, Gender Auditing in Women's Colleges, *University News*, 40(37), Sep. 16-22, 2002.
6. Mallika, R, *Tamil Literature and Feminism–*. New Century Book House (Pvt), Chennai-98.
7. *National Policy On Education-1996*, Programme Of Action Department Of Education, Ministry Of Human Resource Development, Government Of India, New Delhi.
8. Nasrin, *Women in Higher Education*—Challenges of Globalization, AMU, Aligarh.
9. Rohini Sudakar, Education of the Women, *University News*, 40(35), Sep. 2-8, 2002.
10. Santhosh Sharma, Pseudo Gender Equality and the Empowerment of Women, *University News*, 42(38), Sep. 20-26, 2004.

CHAPTER

2

Empowering Women Imparting General and Skill Specific Education

Real Civilization

Poverty and illiteracy are not problems pertaining to India but problems of humanity unless we solve them for the whole world, there will always be trouble such a solution can only mean the ending of poverty and illiteracy and misery everywhere. This may take a long time but we must aim at this and at nothing less than that only then can we have real culture and civilization based on equality. Where there is no exploitation of women or class of any country such a society will be a creative and progressive society adapting itself to changing circumstances and basing itself on the co-operation of its male and female members. And ultimately it must spread all over the world. There will be no danger of such a civilization collapsing or decaying as the old civilizations did.

The Real Disease

Further the real disease of a nation is stagnation not famines or foreign invasions by this exclusiveness the stagnation grew and all avenues of growth are stopped. It is a little dangerous to live in a society which is closed up like a shell. A nation or a state will petrify there and grow unaccustomed to fresh air and fresh ideas. Fresh air is as necessary for societies as for individuals. The fresh air and fresh ideas are now nothing but empowering women in India. If the half of the population of India is women and are illiterates and living in devastatingly poor conditions, India will not claim to have been civilized or cultured. So empowering of Indian women is essential and it is an immediate need.

Women can be empowered only by educating and imparting skills. Education and skills will certainly make them self-reliant and resourceful wherever and whenever they come across problems. They must fully enjoy bargaining power, influencing power, and decision-making power access to resources and have experience of economic and political world.

Until today there is conspicuous absence of principle of shared power between men and women at all levels of activity, became of gender inequality. Equality is a genuine condition for social justice. To promote and render social justice empowering women by all means overcoming hurdles is an imperative. Indian women have immense space to grow into able and capable, and became a social asset. The UNs Millennium goals are also women specific and women oriented to make them live a dignified and expanding life.

Millennium Goals

The UNs first Millennium Goal is to eradicate extreme poverty and hunger by 2015. Specifically the target is to reduce by half the number of people living on less than a dollar a day. The second goal is to achieve universal primary education that is to ensure that all boys and girls complete a full course of primary education. The third is to promote gender equality and empower women, more specifically to dominate gender disparity in primary and secondary education preferably by 2005 and at all levels by 2015.

The fourth goal is a reduction by two-thirds the mortality ratio among children below five. The fifth is to improve maternal health, or reduce by three-quarters the maternal mortality ratio. The sixth goal is to combat and half the spread of HIV/AID, and the incidence of malaria and other diseases. The seventh is to ensure environmental sustainable by integrating principles of sustainable development into country policies and programmes. It also aims at revering the loss of environmental resources, reducing by fifty per cent the proportion of people without success to safe drinking water and achieving significant improvement in likes of at least 100 million slum dwellers by 2020. The eight goal deals with the forging of a global partnership to reduce poverty at the national level, providing decent and productive work for youth. The third the fourth and the fifth goals are clearly women specific and the VN has a great concern for the well being of home makers all over the world.

In India woman is Shakthi. An educated woman is a university. She is everything-both creation and destruction. Status of a woman is a sure indicator of a nation's success. It is desirability but not in real history regard bestowed upon accomplished women is slowly fading. At present they are not enviable members of a family. Frankly speaking they are looked down upon as liabilities.

Other Forces

Despite the fact that daughters are more gracious and caring than sons, they are always treated as a huge and forced commitment. The precarious livelihood of rural people in India, force young mothers to take it for granted the female fortified and infanticide. No mother will like to kill her beloved child, but this is the way they have to live. Their likes and dislikes are determined by other forces, they cannot decide when to mourn, whose death to mourn and how to mourn; these are realities on ground.

The steep fall in the sex ratios in the cities as well envisages and assures that the criminals are within us. We can't blame the poor, ignorant and illiterate and declining sex ratio is part of the most dangerous location for women; that's where she's not allowed to be born, is beaten up, burnt or sexually violated. We are a women hating society. Brining up daughters today is presumed as an expensive affair and women have become permanent refugees in the institution of marriage. India may be known for many things but now it has the distinction of being known as the nation that likes to ensure that girls are never born. The 2001 census figures of 0-6 year's sex ratio are a stark illustration of this reality. We are fasting a national emergency, witnessing a demographic imbalance that will have far reaching social consequences.

There is also an assumption that education and economic independence will help women to assert their rights, including their right to reproductive choice. But a survey by Action India of women in Delhi revealed that even highly educated women have resorted to as many as abortions to ensure that they only give birth to a son. In this country, education and economic progress seem to make no dent or attitudes. On the contrary these are getting more embedded.

Surveys in Haryana and Punjab have revealed that some women genuinely believed that if their numbers decline, their value would increase because men will not find brides. But they buy brides from other states for as little as Rs. 5000. [In Haryana a buffalo costs rupees 40,000!]. These women are available to all the men in the family. Instead of being valued, women are becoming targets of violence and disrespect in districts with lowest sex ratios.

Son preference, sex selection, female fortified, whatever we want it to call is damning indictment of India in the 21st century—Men, women doctors, nurses, health workers, the media, the involved. We boast of our prowess in IT. Yet technology is being misused in this country to fashion a future without women or with a few of them.

Further more in its desire to curtail the growth of population the government has been advocating the two child norm, women's group argue that the combination of son preference and two child norm and wide spread availability sex detection techniques, will ensure the fewer girls will be born in the future.

Economic dependence has rendered millions of women because they are unable to set the terms of relationship with men. Violence and coercion within the marriage and lack of access to property, basic education and employment opportunities are important factors that subjugate women. Governments, Non-governmental organizations, Corporate enterprises, Trusts, Societies all work in various capacities to liberate women and empower them. A kaleidoscopic pasteurization or summary of what is going on in India will enable the reader to visualize the impacts and experiences.

Union Ministry for tribal affairs and state department of tribal welfare (TN) conducted a seminar on 'National Policy for Tribal' in Ooty recently. In this seminar Mr. Kushvarma, Executive Director, Tribal Co-operative Marketing Development Federation of India emphasized that the focus should be on livelihood issues which alone can empower them. The proposed policy should serve as a road map for future. It should give importance to for male and female education, health, intellectual property rights and up lift of primitive tribal groups. The functioning of tribal SHG should be strengthened and help should be extended to them in areas like skill up gradation. He added that the socio-economic development of tribal communities should be accorded top priority.

National Policy

National Policy for Tribals should address the basic issues of the deprived communities. The Forest Conservation Act, 1980 should be amended in such a manner that it would no longer be a hindrance to the scheduled tribal and all the tribal welfare policies should be formulated in consultation with tribal group. Abu Hassan, secretary, state Department of Tribal Welfare urged the Union Government to consider establishing The National Institute of Tribal Research in Ooty. He added that the centre was committed to finalize the National Policy on STs through a process of deliberations consultations and debates on various important issues concerning the tribal. When the 'SHG' scheme was slowly taking root, field staff had to struggle quite a bit. They faced a number of problems in forming the groups and drawing the tribal women who are rationally confined to their homes. Now the confidence of women has grown significantly. They even come to the collect orate on their own initiatives and volition and voice their demands.

Initially the husbands were suspicious and refused to allow the women to attend SHG meetings. But now they find the fund helps them and they are happy, so are there in laws. SHG women feel that funds should reach them directly from the government and not through NGOs, a point to contemplate on. Lives of thousands of women from the under privileged groups have undergone a sea change. SHGs are transforming face of India and strengthening the fabric of gender equity. One can't help being impressed with the change. Cheerful and confident they appear to be the presiding officers of their home making. Economic independence and empowered them to certain extent.

Training in Capacity Building

International Funding Agency for Agricultural Development and 'Mahalirthittam' of Tamil Nadu facilitated many training programmes in Tamil Nadu. Social empowerment, economic empowerment and capacity building are being achieved through series of training programmes such as maintenance of registers, personality and entrepreneur development programmes. A revolving fund helps the members draw from it for medical and education expenses or to meet out marriage commitments and undertake family obligations. Sometimes members turn to it to support their husband's business enterprises. It has inculcated the habit of saving and also provided them with a sense of security. Leadership qualities developed through SHG meetings have seen 2500 women become presidents or members of panchayats and local bodies in Tamilnadu.

The Hindu Succession Act of 1956 granted daughters equal inheritance rights with sons in their father's share of undivided family property. Even after this change, because the notion of coparcenaries of males in the joint family property was left intact. A son could claim his share of the family property by birth and again inherit equally with the daughter the father's share in the family property. By birth right and coparcenaries right a son effectively inherits at least three times as much of the ancestral property as a daughter.

On Equal Footing

It is this inequity that the Law Commission addressed in its report in 2000. It suggested that the Hindu Succession Act should be amended to grant daughters to a right by birth to the Hindu undivided family property. Already Tamil Nadu, Andhra Pradesh, Karnataka and Maharashtra have placed women on an equal footing through amendments to the Hindu Succession Act granting daughters the right by birth to the family property. But Kerala has adopted a more radical course by abolishing the right by birth to the family property altogether. Instead of such state specific laws, the case for an all India law is obvious and brooks no delay. The Law Commission has sent to the Government of India a draft bill to amend the Hindu Succession Act to grant daughters equal coparcenaries right with sons, in joint family property. Ideally, such rights should be enjoyed by all women but law commission recommended that they should be made applicable to women who marry after the new amendment comes into force and not to those who married before the change. But there is no really sound argument why the right should be confined to daughters who marry subsequently.

Right to Agricultural Property

At present in Delhi, Uttar Pradesh, Punjab and Haryana, women do not have the right to agricultural property and the laws in these states have overriding jurisdiction over the Hindu Succession Act. It was therefore necessary to make amendments in the Act to ensure that agricultural property was also covered. This lacuna was brought to the notice of the Union Law Minister, by the Vice President, All India Democratic Women Association.

Indefensible Civil Code

Moreover this demand is surely bound to raise the demand for the reform of all personal laws that discriminate against women, more specifically Muslim personal law. However without waiting for a uniform civil code gross gender discrimination that persists in all personal laws needs to be addressed as priority. A readiness to reform can be created by a dialogue and debate addressing the laws that discriminate against women grossly and are indefensible. Union and State Government agencies and NGOs have found that it is very difficult to root out child labour. Poverty and broken homes contribute to it. Parents abandon the children when they remarry and are left in the care of their grandmothers. Female children as usual get exploited more as child labour. False certificates are obtained about their age. The nexus between the guardians and factory owners is strong and cunning evading the preventive measures that have been imposed. Despite this kind of practical difficulties the agencies are preserving. Kovai CLASS (Child Labour Abolition Support Society) nearly rescued 1600 child worker both boys and girls, from different parts of the district. They were all immediately in the 50 special centers run by Kovai CLASS. They were provided learning materials free of cost and would be helped to join regular schools after a year. The rehabilitated children were unable to attend special centers regularly. Some of the rescued child workers were either from remote areas or their parents were migratory labourers. Kovai CLASS felt the need and has proposed to start residential schools especially for those from remote areas. The schools will be run with the assistance under SSA scheme. Initially each residential school would have 50 children aged between 8 and 14. After six months they would be assisted to join regular schools. They would also be provided food free of cost.

A Daunting Task

The Sarva Siksha Abhiyan (SSA) is a Government of India project for universal elementary education in partnership with the states under the Tenth Five Year Plan. This is a time bound target to be achieved by 2010. In a country as diverse as ours educating all the 192 million children could be a daunting task. Providing quality education with life skills within the total budget of Rs. 1800 crore is a challenging goal. To achieve this we require innovative models. Cost effective approaches need to be adopted to build capabilities of teachers. Relevant and productive, education, especially girl child who is the first drop out of school, has to be provided too.

The Avinashilingam Jan Shikshan Sansthan is one of the oldest institutions in the country. It provides need based and skill-oriented training to tribal's, women *dalits* and neo-literates to make them economically independent. K.R. Chandra Sekaran Assistant Educational Advisor, Ministry of Human Resource Development, Department of Elementary education and literacy, Government of India recently took part in a programme to train the teachers under this project. He expressed his ambition that local resources need to be tapped to implement the goals of SSA.

For instance 576 teachers have been trained in art education. Skills such as doll making, gift article making and glass painting have been imparted. These teachers become resource persons, to train students in their local schools, especially girl children. This type of training is district specific (Coimbatore specific). It is productive and cost effective and helps teachers to create "joyful learning in their class rooms apart from teaching skills that can be used later."

One of the major goals of SSA is to main stream the school drop outs K.R. Chandra Sekaran sees this model an effective one. This model should be replicated in other states too and already Karnataka is showing interest in learning from this experience. The survey of child labour in Coimbatore District in 2003 has identified 2573 child labours of these 1301 are girls. How could the programme bring such children under the SSA purview? Under the scheme there are various options for flexible education. One such scheme is the educational guarantee scheme, which provides local teachers for every ten students in areas where child labour is prevalent. In 1995 the Child Labour Elimination Society (CLES) was formed in Dumka, in Jharkhand state. In dumka, the literacy level was characteriscally low and child labour too rampant. CLES prepared a detailed plan to run 40 Bal Shramik Vidyalaya in three blocks—Jarmundi, Saraiyahaat and Jamtara respectively. The CLES was meant to ensure the smooth functioning of the BSVs.

There are many practical difficulties in running the schools unlike regular schools, these special schools have children of different age groups in the classes and special attention is given to each child to make up for the years it has lost. Another problem is the non-availability of books which forces parents to buy books out of the monthly stipend. The parents find it very difficult to sustain their children's education, because most of the children studying in these schools belong to the scheduled caste, scheduled tribe and backward castes. These BSVs faction in an effort to draw a majority of the child labour population into mainstream education.

In a unique effort, parents of child labourers monitor the functioning of BSVs based on three counts—serving of the midday meal, regular health check up for students and attendance of teachers. Despite the hiccups, the Jamtara experience is expected to go a long way in eliminating illiteracy and child labour in the country. In a study conducted in Common Wealth countries on women in higher positions, India ranked the lowest. There are only 20 per cent or fewer women managers in the university system. Alarmed, the UGC has undertaken a countrywide initiative to train women academicians to go beyond academics into university management. Though a series of gender sensitization and competence building workshops VGC hopes to create a cadre of change agents. Explaining reasons for sparse participation of women, Jaya Indiresan who is training teachers on academic leadership has identified three key factors. There is gender bias in the system. There are socio cultural factors that create conflicting priorities of balancing home and work and finally there are capability issues.

Local Government is essentially the empowerment of the people by giving them not only the voice, but the power of choice as well as in order to shape the development which they feel is appropriate to their situation. Institutions such as hospitals and schools that have a bearing on everyday life in rural communities including in agriculture animal husbandry, fisheries micro irrigation and small scale industrial sectors are still under the jurisdiction of local self Government Institutions.

A New Civic Culture

Development can be equitable and effective only if people control the process themselves. Therefore vital to the success of the programme was the 'generation of a new civic culture' involving large scale participation of people (SHGs) in the grama-sabhas. In the Panchayats SHGs intervention has been effective the experience has been rewarding in Kerala. State

Poverty Eradication Mission Kudumbshree self-help groups have utilized the opportunities provided by the centralized Local Government Institutions to the lilt. It is a sparkling example. Well-run women SHGs, participate in the grama-sabha a forum where they came prepared to argue for what they want and get. 'Kudambashree' SHGs supported by the Mission were able to provide income, employment and enterprise to so many of poor disadvantaged women in the state only in the context of decentralization. Decentralization offered 'Kudumbshree' SHGs the opportunity of accessing funds from several sources through Panchayats. The decentralized Panchayats offered a myriad empowerment opportunities and Kudumbashree helped to target them to the needy.

Kudambashree have played a responsible role in decentralization in Kerala ensuring participation in the grama-sabhas helping Panchayats through meticulous and rational selection of beneficiaries and by setting directions for the decentralization process itself leading it to hitherto unattended sectors Kerala society. The Kudumbashree taps 75 per cent of its resources from the funds of decentralized Local Self Government Institutions (LSGI) meant for poor women and targets it to the needy through its women SHGs that functions almost as a voluntary mini-grama sabhas for beneficiary selection.

AIDS

More than 20 million people had died of AIDS since the discovery of the disease in the late 70s. About 40 million people have been living with HIV full blown AIDS at the end of the year 2003 of the 5 million new infections in 2003, about half were among young people aged between 15 and 24 of these almost 60 per cent were young women. AIDS had orphaned more than 14 million children, currently under the age of 15. In India there are six high prevalence states—Tamil Nadu, Maharashtra, Andhra Pradesh, West Bengal, Nagaland

and Manipur. About half of the total HIV infected was women. Many women and girls were vulnerable to HIV because of the high risk behaviour of others. It is well-known that quite often men who buy enforce women to ignore safe-practices such as condom use. Women are unable to negotiate safe sex within marriage or outside for a variety of reasons.

Stigma and Discrimination

Women living with HIV suffer a lot; lack of social and economic influence increases the risk violence against these women—neglect, denial, violation of rights—these factors manifest differently in the way they apply to men and women. Stigma and discrimination appeared on top of the list of problems, they are facing. Negatively impacted by humiliation at both individual level within the marital and natal home and lack of programmatic responses from the state have driven them to destitution. When her positive status came to be known, let down by all agencies she found herself out on a limb.

Significant Concerns

Since there is life even after infection, HIV+ women has every right to live with dignity and respect. A study carried out by a U.N. agency identified six significant concerns that need placing within a right discourse.

The concerns are:

1. Health care and treatment
2. Property Succession and inheritance within natal and marital homes
3. Access to productivity rights
4. Healthy livelihood opportunities
5. Decision-making powers and
6. Access to state sponsored benefits.

The study also highlights the relevance of the provisions of the convention "On the elimination of all forms discrimination against women" that upholds the civil and legal status of women and the accountability of Governments to ensure that. It also contends that the constitution embodies many of these rights which can be read directly or implicitly. It is a matter of deep concern that many state facilitated programmes even on world AIDS day forgot to create space for people living with HIV.

ABC Approach

India has promised anti retroviral treatment for all those who need it. But it can ill-afford to add greater number of people to the scheme. The ABC approach to prevention Abstinence, Being faithful and reducing the number of sexual partners and condom use will have only a limited impact if the underlying socio-economic and cultural causes are not addressed. Protecting women and girls from HIV/AIDS generally is an effort in which everyone has a part to play. The American people are privileged to join the people of India. We will work together to turn the tide against HIV/AIDS. In a study on trafficking in women and female children in India 2002-03, commissioned by the National Human Rights Commission (NHRC) 4000 persons involved in some way or other in commercial sex were interviewed. Among the victims of sexual exploitation, Andhra Pradesh accounted for 29.5 per cent of the girls, Karnataka 15 per cent, West Bengal 12.5 per cent and Tamil Nadu 12.3 per cent. Another study done by Chennai Indian Community Welfare Organisation among 300 sex workers in May 2002, established that 55 per cent of all commercial sex workers in the city had come from Andhra Pradesh, followed by 11 per cent from Kerala.

The Most Affected

Either way commercial sex is not a healthy practice. The most affected and infected are women partners. HIV/AIDS originate from the premises of commercial sex. Women living abject poverty are not able to understand the repercussions of commercial sex. To them it is a death trap. Agriculture diversification and promotion of rural non-farm sector are important for employment generation. Diversification from food crops to non-food crops and allied activities can increase employment. Rural employment could prevent women migration to towns and cities, where they have to counter many traps for a decent placement. But often many young women are lead astray by the antisocial elements. Union and state Governments should give full, equal and sustained attention to the human rights of women in the exercise of their respective mandates to promote universal respect for and protection of all human rights. Governments should monitor and ensure that there is co-ordination and collaboration of the work of all human rights bodies and mechanisms. It is important to provide training in the human rights of women for all personal and officials especially those in human rights and humanitarian relief activities. It is also essential to promote their understanding of the human rights of women and can fully take into account the gender aspect of their work.

Commendatory Status

At present national or state Human Rights Commission could not intervene more effectively. One of the basic problems of the commissions formed as per (Central Human) Rights Act was that they had only commendatory status. There is no enforcement agency for the commission and its recommendations may or may not be implemented. Similarly the commission cannot insist that a person appear before it. The commission can send summons to the person, but if he or she refuses to appear before the commission, there is not much it could do. There is provision in the Human Rights Act that one Court of Session in every district shall be designated as human rights court. The recommendations of NHRC and SHRCs can be pursued as cases in those courts by registering them as FIRs.

The designation of a court in the district as human rights court is to be done by the High Court and only then can prosecutors can be appointed. Globalization will be a misnomer, if inequalities between the rich and poor nations and unequal distribution of wealth between them are making the life of poor especially poor women miserable. Liberty and freedom has no real value for the rural poor illiterate and unemployed. How could we create a healthy society when 85 per cent of the pregnant women are anemic?

From the experience of many developing and developed countries, it is learned that may small-scale industries generate most jobs, through income generating activities. Only the improvement in rural economy will eliminate malnutrition and anemic conditions of women especially pregnant women. Regular counselling by women health workers with reference to nutrition with reference to nutrition and food habits also will go a long way in the process of reducing the number of anemic women whom we need to empower.

It is clearly seen that in a vast country such as India a multicultural and multilevel approach is inevitable to perform the task of empowering millions of women. Fortunately in India there is no dearth of service minded people, agencies, trusts, societies, organizations, corporate who contribute to the supply side of the task 'The poor, unprivileged and tribal women form the demand side, though vulnerable.' If the supply side and the demand side understand each other and work together, shouldering mutually the daunting task of empowering women will surely been achieved before long, with the facilitation of union and state Governments.

CHAPTER

3

Leadership Quality for Women Through ICT

Introduction

India has changed its image from a country of snake charmers to—High tech mouse movers. Neither a man nor a woman is complete by himself or herself. From birth to death they have to play a complementary role. He completes her, she completes him. If a woman grows up unlettered it certainly tells up on her family. If a man grows up illiterate his family is ruined. Untold miseries creep into the family. It is in this context learned men all over the world emphasize that women must learn and lead an educated life, supporting the endeavour and efforts of her husband throughout their life. If she happens to live alone due to misfortunes, education empowers her to live a dignified life.

Ascribed to Achieved

Moreover growth and development of the society cannot take place as long as women are not educated. Realizing this, policy planners and educationists initiated several policies and programmes to promote the educational level of girls and governments offer free education up to the university level. The government also provides 33 per cent employment opportunities for women. This offer encouraged girls' students to enroll in great numbers in all levels of educational institutions and there is a visible change in the status of women from ascribed to accomplished.

Thanks to Information and Communication Technology. ICT Distance Education and Open Universities have been made more meaningful and dimensional. Higher education is more accessible to all girls irrespective of their living places. ICT abolished the myth of gender bias and sex stereotyping and has made the curriculum at all stages of education gender sensitive and gender friendly to achieve gender justice, gender harmony and gender peace. Now a day, women are very active in India as well as in the foreign countries as effective-dynamic computer professionals.

Being exposed to ICT, girls' involvement in vocational and technical programmes, giving up traditional courses, is highly encouraging and rewarding to the nation. They easily learn new skills and technology. Taking into account the spontaneous involvement of the girls, a new scheme 'Technology for women' was introduced in the universities during 1998-99 for providing financial assistance for introducing U.G courses in engineering and technology. In addition to this hundred more ITIs with women's wings were set up.

Whether it is technical or non technical, whether it is classical or non-classical, whether it is traditional or non-traditional learning, whether it is for boys or for girls, ICT does not discriminate. One remarkable and splendid feature of ICT is its transcending capabilities of all physical and spiritual barriers. The transcending nature and feature of ICT enabled the girl students to learn a lot and differently. ICT media has made learning cognitive, comfortable, personalized, individualized, optional, and collaborative and cross disciplinary. Comfortable learning is a boon to girl students. They learn anything anytime and anywhere. ICT media gives self-confidence among the girls in the competitive world.

ICT literacy is not confined to time and age. It provides for lifelong education. The fast changing nature of occupations demands lifelong education. It requires a passionate ICT literacy to live well placed. Private firms or enterprising companies and corporations prefer a woman candidate to a male candidate. By gradual emancipation and empowerment through ICT education, it is proved that women are no more a stagnant part of a dynamic society. The women have been creating a digital empowerment in the world and will do so in the coming years too.

Decades ago Indian women lived in isolated conditions, looking after the children and minding the household duties. Interpenetration of electronic devices leads to media fusion. A healthy media fusion has evolved a media culture. Either at home or at working place girls are exposed to media culture or they feel conveniently and comfortable at receiving ends. Easy liberal and lenient access to ICT education has broken the barrier of isolation and dependence.

With ubiquitous presence of electronic media, in and out, the school atmosphere reaches out to all students. A girl student learning a skill is a survival. ICT literacy is no more a survival skill to the women community in India. Now a day's ICT literate women, though a few are emerging as a challenge to men in all departments and firms.

Though the percentage of ICT literate women is lagging behind the percentage of men, it does not cut a sorry figure. If all the government departments work expeditiously, exhaustively, coherently and pin-pointedly with the educational insti-tutions, ICT literacy rate of Indian women will certainly be enhanced in the coming years.

Without health, a human being can do nothing. Sound mind and sound body are very essential. Even educated women do not know how to wear dress, inner dryers etc. a healthy family is the wealth of a country.

Using ICT Technology, a woman can learn the following:

- Hygienic food making,
- Hygienic dress wearing,
- Hygienic pregnancy,
- Hygienic nursing,
- Hygienic child nourishment,
- Hygienic child care,
- Hygienic housekeeping.

Thus, it is high time women need to have IT literacy to lead her family in a wealthier way, with a healthy environment.

Earth an Eden

By virtue of being a woman, she is the first teacher of her child. Teaching and nursing are quite instinctive. An Indian woman who has ICT literacy will certainly think globally and act locally. A well informed motherly outlook and attitude with ICT literacy will no doubt make our earth an Eden. Women are the building blocks of the good nation.

REFERENCES

1. *University News* 41(11), March 17-23, 2003.
2. Hilt S.R., and Well Man, (1977), Asynchronous Learning Networks as Virtual Classroom, Communication of the ACM 4d(s).
3. *University News* 40(20) May 20-26, 2002.
4. *University News* 40(28), July 15-21, 2002.

CHAPTER

4

Portrait of the Women in the Policy and Government

Man is turn to perform duties and woman is made to bear the responsibilities, Bearing a child is a responsible talk and job and hence it is given to the woman for their politeness, humbleness and tolerance.

The Hindu belief according to Puranas is that Lord Shiva treating Parvathi his equal part showed his own body with her and still it could be seen at Arthanareeswaran Temple at Thiruchengodu (Salem District, Tamilnadu) and in the words of our National poet. Sri Subramanya Bharathi, "It is Breast feeding giving strength, it is to feculence brings dignity to life". Even eve was made with a heal cause of sharing the joy of the world.

Being given adequate of duties women have shown that they can venture into any field and come out successful and History, Politics, Science, Medicine, Literature, Sports, Arts, Dance, Education field have got woman stalwarts or part with men and on a few occasions women have excelled men. Women were considered as an integral and inseparable part of the family and men. Many a battles had also been forget for women.

But the dawn of modern civilization instead of uplifting the status of woman started to erode their importance and tried to confine them into four walls for household affairs only. Notwithstanding the tendency of men folk all over the world, persons like Rajaram Mohan Roy and poets of Subramaniya Bharathi rose to the up-liftment women and to the world witnesses the International women's day on March 8th.

Post independence period has seen a good many members of steps towards women's development especially eradica-ting illiteracy among women have taken up. The constitution of India adopted on 26th January 1950 had fourteen women members in the constituent Assembly and it not only provides equality to women but also empowers the state to take any special measures to centralize the cumulative social, economic, educational and political disadvantage of centuries.

In addition to fundamental rights to women, the constitution of India provided many directive principles of state policy addressing women. The fundamental rights justifiable in the court of law given in the constitution of India are given below.

Article 14: Confers a men and women equal rights and opportunities in the political economic and social spheres.

Article 15: Prohibits discrimination against any citizen as the grounds of religion, race, caste and sex.

Article 15 (3): Makes a special provision enabling the state to make affirmative discrimination in favour of women.

Article 15 (A) (e): Imposes a fundamental duty as every citizen to renounce practices derogatory to the dignity of women.

Article 16: Provides for equality of opportunities in matter of public appointment for all children.

Article 39(a): The state shall direct its policy towards securing all citizens, men and women, equally, the right to means of livelihood.

Article 39 (e): Directs the state to ensure equal pay for equal work.

Article 42: Dinettes the state to ensure just and humane conditions of work and maternity relief.

Article 44: A uniform civil code for the citizen.

Article 45: Free and compulsory education to all children up to the age of fourteen within ten years of the coming into force of the constitution.

Article 47: The state is further committed to raising the nutritional levels, health and living standards of the people.

To put it and track, the equal Remuneration Act of 1976. The Hindu Marriage Act of 1955 providing the right for a girl to repudiate a child marriage before attaining maturity whether the marriage has been consummated or not, and the right to property entitling her to make a "will" leaving shave of property and absolute ownership over the property to her heirs. The Immoral Traffic (prevention) Act of 1956, the Dowry Prohibition Act of 1961, the Factories Act of 1948 (amended up to 1976) (Providing for establishment of create when 30 women are employed) and the Medical Termination of Pregnancy any Act of 1971 have been passed.

A new enactment of Indecent Representation of woman (prohibition) Act of 1986 and the Commission of Sati (prevention) Act, 1987 have also been passed to protect the dignity of women and prevent violence against then as well as their exploitation. To make it more effective the 73rd and 74th Constitutional Amendments (1992) give 33 per cent representation to women in panchayats and Nagar Palikas and 30 per cent leaderships to women in these bodies at the village, block and district levels in neural areas and in towns and cities and in addition to the above some significant laws for children in India. The employment of Children Act, 1938. The Factories Act, 1948, the Beedi and cigar workers Act, 1966. The children (Pledying of labour) Act, 1933. The child marriage restraint Act of 1929 amended in 1976, to raise the minimum age of marriage for girls from 15 to 18 years and for boys from 18 to 21 years have also been enacted.

Several states have passed compulsory primary education Acts. The UN general assembly adapted Convention as the Elimination of all forms of Discrimination (CEDAW) Against Women on 18th December 1979 and India is also a signatory and in addition to above laws. Based on the UN declaration of the Right of the child. India and its states have also come forward with special plans on child welfare and they have taken important measures to:

(*a*) Recognize that every child has the interest right to life;

(*b*) Provides the child the right to freedom of thought;

(*c*) Provide equal opportunity free and compulsory primary education.

A hallmark of the 1980's and 1990's in the growth of move and better information on woman coming in through research-cum-Activities efforts and the size of women's studies to analysis, generate and supports Action.

The major policy shifts have taken place in our country are given below:

(*a*) From macro, aggregative, centralized planning to disaggregate decentralized micro planning with people's participation;

(*b*) From welfare to development and finally empowerment of women;

(*c*) From women's concerns to issue of the girl child;

(*d*) From seeing girls education only as a commitment to viewing it as a sound investment.

To achieve this equality we will have to ensure that,

(*a*) She has the right to survive;

(*b*) She has the right to be free from poverty, hunger, ignorance and exploitation;

(*c*) She has the right to equality, dignity, freedom, opportunity, care, protection and development and finally;

(*d*) She has the right to enjoy the above right.

Teachers and educational administrators—males and females—coming from the same cultural miliev as the pupils, hence also unconsciously internalized not only the traditional division of labour in the family but also male superiority and make entitlement to a larger than of family resources even by use of force.

In India what are all found in the letters are not found in the spirit. "Right can be declared and policies can be formulated to express our collective literal and humanistic concern but unless the real life of the girl child in her family and the community by tangible efforts and Actions, nothing can be achieved. Therefore, a climate has to be created in which she can exercise her rights freely and fearlessly". (National Plan of Action for SAARC Decade of the girl child 1991-2000).

As in evident there is a clear mandate for social mobilization to change the social and cultural practices that inhibit the development of the girl child. For planning suitable strategies and interventions it would be necessary to briefly review the present factual position regarding the girl child and the existing efforts at social mobilization.

REFERENCES

1. National Policy on Education (1986): Ministry of Human Resource and Development, Govt. of India, 1986.
2. Government of India: Census of India, 1991.
3. Ministry of Education, Challenge of Education (1985).
4. A Paradigm for Women and Child Development, *Indian Economic Panorama*, April 1999.

CHAPTER

5

Education for Women's Empowerment

An Evaluation of the Government Run Schemes to Educate the Girl Child

Introduction

Women and men in India enjoy de jure equality. Article 14 of the Constitution of India guarantees equal rights and opportunities to men and women in political, economic and social spheres, Article 42 directs the State to make provision for ensuring just and humane conditions for work and maternity itself and Article 51 (A) e imposes upon every citizen, a fundamental duty to renounce the practices derogatory to the dignity of women. However this de jure equality has not yet materialised into a de facto equality, despite the efforts made in the Five Year Plans. The First Five Year Plan sought to "promote the welfare of women" by helping them to play their legitimate role in the family and the community but emphasised that the major burden of organising activities for the benefit of the female population had to be borne by the private agencies. Five Year Plans continued to reflect the same welfare approach to women's interests though they accorded priority to education for both, men and women and launched measures to improve maternal and child health services and supplementary nutrition for children as well as expectant and nursing mothers.

It was the Sixth Five Year Plan in which the focus on women's interests shifted from 'welfare' and 'development'. Planners and policy-makers began to recognize women not only as partners but also as stake-holders in the development of the country. The Seventh Five Year Plan saw developmental programmes which aimed at raising the economic and social status of women and at ensuring that they get the benefits of national development. This is when 'beneficiary oriented programmes' extending direct benefits to women in different developmental sectors began. There was a stress upon the generation of both skilled and unskilled employment through formal and non-formal education and vocational training. The Eight Five Year Plan had a Human Development focus. It tried to ensure that the benefits of development do not bypass women and it implemented special programmes for women to complement the general development programmes and to monitor the flow of benefits to women in education, health and employment.

The Ninth Five Year Plan was rather ambitious. It took up 'empowering women as agents of socio-economic change and development' as a major commitment. To begin with, it adopted the 'National Policy for Empowerment of Women', which among other objectives, sought to organise women into Self Help Groups to work for their own empowerment, accorded a high priority to schemes for maternal and child welfare and most importantly, made a bid at easy and equal access to education through the Special Action Plan of 1998, plans for the free education of girls up to the college level (inclusive of professional courses) and vocational training.

Education as such, results in positive externalities. Not only does it have an intrinsic value in the sense of the joy of learning, reading etc, but it also has instrumental, social and process roles. Moreover education may spread through interpersonal motivation. When one individual sends her child to school, her neighbour is likely to do so as well. Women's education too, often spreads this way, more specifically, through same sex effects. *i.e.*, an educated woman is far more likely to send her daughter to school than an uneducated woman. Also, she is likely to maintain better conditions of nutrition and hygiene in her household and thereby improve her family's health (Sen 1997). The presence of a larger number of female teachers may encourage parents to send their daughters to school. Thus education is a fundamental tool for women's empowerment.

In this chapter, I have taken up the girls' education schemes of the Ministry of Human Resource Development and the Ministry of Women and Child Development and I have evaluated them with respect to their public policy design in terms of aims, objectives and implementation tactics with reference to the extent to which they involve the grassroots. Prior to the evaluation of the schemes however, I have provided statistics representing the extent of gender inequality in current and initial enrolment, literacy and retention, listed variables that have been statistically proven to increase girls' enrolment and given a few reports on education for empowerment.

Vital Statistics

The Report of the Taskforce on Education for Women's Equality shows that while males exceeded females by 32 million, illiterate females exceeded their male counterparts by as much as 70 million. (CSO 1991) There was a significant rural-urban divide in female literacy. On approximation, rural female literacy was half of that of the urban areas.

Dropout rates were significant. In rural areas, for every 100 girls in Class I, there were 40 in Class V, 18 in Class VIII, 9 in Class IX and only 1 in Class XII. The corresponding figures for urban areas were 82, 62, 32 and 14, respectively.

The Report of the Taskforce on Education for Women's Equality also suggests that for greater female enrolment and retention, the presence of female teachers at the primary level is useful. In lieu of Table 5.1, it can be seen that while merely 21 per cent of primary school teachers in rural areas were female, 56 per cent was the corresponding figure in urban areas. This can be a significant reason for the lower dropout rates and higher enrolment rates of girls in urban areas. It is understandable that parents might be wary of sending their daughters to a school without female teachers.

Fig. 5.1 : No. of Girl Students for 100 Girl Students in Class I, 1991.

	Class V	Class VIII	Class IX	Class XII
Rural Areas	40	18	9	1
Urban Areas	82	62	32	14

Source: MHRD, The Report of the Taskforce on Education for Women's Equality.

Infrastructure, teachers and enrolment: Efforts towards attaining Universal Elementary Education (UEE) have resulted in a substantial increase in physical infrastructure, teachers and enrolment. The number of primary schools had increased from 0.642 million to 0.767 million between 1999 and 2005. The number of teachers in Primary Schools had increased from 1.91 million in 1999 to 2.31 million in 2004-5 and enrolment had increased from 113.61 million to 131.69 million in the same period. It is intuitive that a lower Student-Teacher Ratio facilitates enrolment as teachers can now give more attention to each student. The increase in enrolment for girls at the primary level was 5.2 per cent in this period-far higher than 1.7 per cent for boys, according to The Chapter on Elementary Education of the Working Group Report for the Eleventh Five Year Plan.

As per the quality of schools, according to the Working Group Report, the percentage of schools having girls' toilets on campus has increased from 28.24 per cent in 2003-4 to 37.42 per cent in 2005-6. This is still dismal. Not having a girls' toilet in school would mean that girls often skip class to go to far-off toilets. This clearly decreases the quality of schooling. In Bihar merely 11.78 per cent of schools had a girls' toilet as late as 2005-6. The proportion of schools without female teachers has gone down from 35.72 per cent in 2003-4 to 30.87 per cent in 2005.

Underlying Statistics

Gautam Bhan in his report to Swedish International Development Agency, titled India Gender Profile, makes it clear that while the Census of India, 2001 may report a 15 per cent rise in female literacy (higher than 13.2% for males), it does not imply an improvement in gender bias in education. Thanks to the unbalanced sex ratio, an increase of 15 per cent in female literates implies an increase of merely 10.51 million in contrast to 21.4 million male literates. In Bihar, the number of female illiterates actually rose by 12.25 per cent a drastic increase of 2.31 million illiterate persons over the 1990's. In fact the number of female illiterates rose in 10 states and union territories. In Rajasthan in 2001, only 4 per cent of SC women were literate. However, Rajasthan reported an increase of 1 million female literates over the 1990's. 19 per cent of SC females were literate in 1991 and 18 per cent was the corresponding figure for ST females. Data for 2001 is, unfortunately not available.

Bhan does acknowledge that there were some positive features in the gender education scenario. Gender gap between male and female literacy fell from 24.85 per cent in 1991 to 21.68 per cent in 2001. However, he notes that gender gap is consistent through higher schooling. While the Gross Enrolment Ratio (GER) was as high as 92.7 per cent for girls in 1992-3, merely 53.8 per cent of girls went on for secondary schooling.

GER is often inaccurate and inflated, especially during what Bhan calls the 'enrolment session'. Instead, data on current enrolment should be relied upon. Bhan points out that current enrolment was merely 32.2 per cent for rural females in contrast to 70 per cent for urban females and 46.4 per cent for rural males. The corresponding figure for urban males was 76.9 per cent.

A Cursory Look at Causes of Gender Bias

Reasons for low enrolment and retention of girls, according to Gautam Bhan, are early marriages. 4.3 per cent of girls between 10 and 14 and 35.3 per cent of girls between 15 and 19 are married (Bhan 2001). In urban areas, it is recognized that education increases a girl's marriage ability while in rural areas; education implies that a girl lacks domestic skills and will make a bad wife. The opportunity costs of a girl's time are also very high as she has domestic responsibilities of sibling care etcetera, especially if her mother is working.

This is also because it is considered suitable to marry a girl off to a social superior. An educated girl should be married off to a more educated man. The more education a girl gets, the more difficult (and expensive) it is to find her a groom. Moreover the fact that a girl must leave her parents' home and sometimes village, once she gets married, reduces a parent's incentive to send her child to school. Sending a girl to school is like 'watering someone else's plant', according to popular perception. (Sen and Dreze 2002) The results of the PROBE survey by Jean Dreze and Geeta Kingdon show the various other factors that have been statistically shown to influence the school participation of a girl child.

Variables known to Increase Girls' School Participation

In 'School Participation in Rural India' Dreze and Kingdon deny the conventional wisdom that low school participation occurs due to parental indifference. Qualitative data from the PROBE survey in the four most educationally backward states—Bihar, Madhya Pradesh, Rajasthan and Uttar Pradesh suggests that almost 90 per cent of parents would like to send their children to school, particularly boys. As far as girls are concerned, the probability that a girl will be enrolled in a school goes up by 30 per cent if her parents believe that a girl should go to school. "Parents are not generally opposed to female education but they are reluctant to pay for it." This implies that State intervention in the form of free text books, uniforms etcetera can be an important factor in the initial enrolment of a girl child.

Also, the PROBE survey suggests that child labour isn't such a potent cause of low school participation in India. It claims that an out-of-school child works only two hours more than a child who attends school. As such, the PROBE Survey classifies the variables that affect a child's participation in school into household, school and village characteristics. The Household variables include parental education, ownership of cows and goats, dependency ratio, caste and religion. The regression co-efficient of these variables against initial and current enrolment of girls had tested significant and had the expected signs.

1. Parental education increased enrolment sharply.
2. Cross sex effects were not as strong as same sex effects. It was seen that a mother's education did not significantly affect her son's probability of enrolment but it increased the probability that her daughter would be initially and currently enrolled.
3. The ownership of cows and goats decreased the probability of a girl's enrolment. This was because the daughter of the household would be expected to milk the cows and feed the cattle.
4. There was an inverse relationship between the dependency ratio and the probability that a girl child would be enrolled. This is due to sibling care responsibilities that would inevitably fall upon the girl child—especially if her mother was working.
5. It was also seen that being an SC/ST and a girl decreased an individual's chance of being enrolled

by 8 per cent in contrast to 6 per cent in case of being an OBC and a girl. Muslim girls were not found to be significantly less likely to be enrolled in a school.

While school variables like the successful implementation of the Mid-Day Meal Scheme, proper infrastructure, teacher regularity and child teacher ratio did not significantly affect boys' initial and current enrolment, they tested significant for girls.

1. The presence of the mid-day meal increased the probability that a girl would be enrolled by 15 per cent. This was because it reduced the per-capita costs of schooling.
2. A lower child teacher ratio meant higher enrolment of girls as did teacher regularity.
3. This is possibly because a low value of such variables would decrease the benefit of schooling which would then be lower than the high opportunity cost of a girl's time (sibling care, housework etcetera).
4. School infrastructure tested negative—this is counter intuitive but Dreze and Kingdon explain it by stating that the PROBE survey was targeted at villages where school participation was unusually low and less likely to be affected by better infrastructure.

Village variables too were shown to affect girls' enrolment.

1. The village development index tested positive for girls, which is understandable, considering that a more progressive village would be more likely to cause girls to go to school.
2. The presence of a women's association in the village was also seen to increase girls' enrolment.

The PROBE Survey shows that a programme or a scheme to increase the enrolment and retention rates of the girl child should account for all possible factors. The per capita costs of schooling should be reduced due to the high opportunity costs of a girl's time. Therefore, the provision of midday meals and cheap text books are important. To increase retention rates however, the presence of a female teacher, or at least a gender sensitized teacher, the presence of a girls' toilet, a lower child teacher ratio and regular teaching is essential-partly to increase the benefit of schooling and to guard against gender insensitive remarks and actions.

However, high enrolment is possible even in the absence of these conditions. According to 'First Class against All Odds' by Rajat K Panda, the Swastik School, a remote institution without electricity in Godbhanga village, has no school drop outs and 22 first class students out of 34. Schools in the area have low retention rates and poor academic records. Panda attributes its success to the perseverance of the headmaster.

Every school may not have one and the experience of this school need not be replicable. Yet, the Swastik School has met with its outstanding results also because it has rendered hostel facilities and because it has mobilized the children around a cause protecting the sale forest behind their school. There are policy implications in the first clause. The second will be difficult for the government to replicate. However, it proves that scope for a greater participation by the local community can also further enrolment and grade attainment. With these factors in mind, I shall in the course of this paper, evaluate various Centrally sponsored education schemes like the Sarva Shiksha Abhiyan, KGBV, ICDS and others to empower the girl child.

Centrally Sponsored Schemes (CSS) for the Education of the Girl Child and Adolescent Girls

The United Progressive Alliance had pledged in its Common Minimum Programme to empower women politically, educationally, economically and legally to ensure gender equality. The Tenth Five Year Plan had an overly ambitious target of reducing gender gaps in literacy by at least 50 per cent in 2007. Even the Mid-Term Appraisal of the Plan conceded that the target was unrealistic. According to the 2006-07 Budget Rs. 222.51 billion was to be spent exclusively for women. Schemes in which all the beneficiaries were women were to receive 100 per cent of their funding from this fund while those which benefited women indirectly were to get 30 per cent. However, even schemes like the India Awas Yojana in which only 77.17 per cent of the beneficiaries are women and the National Child Labour Project in which only 44 per cent of the expenditure is exclusively for girls have been given 100 per cent of their funding from the fund that is to be used exclusively for women.

Schemes for the empowerment of girls and women can be classified into schemes for (1) livelihood generation; (2) education; (3) health; (4) food security and nutrition; (5) housing; and (6) protection and the generation of awareness. Education schemes have had the largest budgetary allocation of the fund for women's empowerment. It was as high as 38 per cent in 2006-07 and is still 31 per cent of the total in the 2007-8 Budget. A major chunk of the allocation for the education of girls and women has been accorded to the Ministry of Human Resource Development's Sarva Shiksha Abhiyan (SSA). In absolute terms, Rs. 50.6 billion was being spent on the SSA in 2006-07.

Funding Pattern for Centrally Sponsored Schemes

One of the troubles with the Centrally Sponsored Schemes including those for the education of girls and women is their system of disbursement of funds. This process is highly complicated and involves a step by step transfer of funds and release orders. First the Pay and Accounts Officer of the department concerned in the Government of India (*e.g.*, The Department of Elementary Education and Literacy of the Ministry of Human Resource Development) sends release orders for CSS funds to the Central Accounting System (CAS) set up by the Reserve Bank of India in Nagpur. Also, it sends a release order to the corresponding administrative department at the State level. The CAS then sends a release order to the State Financial Department while the State Administrative Department sends release orders to the State Treasury and the District Account. Finance Departments of states often make implementing departments bring them copies of release orders and don't release funds otherwise. Release orders slowly filter down to the District Account, Block Account, Village Account and finally to the payees. Funds too are transferred in this tedious way. The CAS releases funds to the State Treasury which sends them down to the District Account which in turn transmits them to the Block Account which then dispatches them to the Village Account which ultimately releases them to the payees.

The paragraph above has been summed up diagrammatically in Figure 5.2. It is far too complex to visualize or even understand otherwise. Needless to say, this complicated procedure causes funds to be 'parked' or delayed at various levels and that the complication is a fantastic cover-up for corruption and for the siphoning of funds.

Overall function was rated 'poor' according to the survey team	13	32	41	42
Supplementary nutrition was not being provided	0	9	13	25
Percentage of villages in which:	—	—	—	—
Motivation of mothers to send their children to school was 'high' or 'very nhigh'	60	55	29	23

Fig. 5.4 : Statewide Comparison of Anganwadi Centres on the basis of the FOCUS Survey.

Source: Adapted from Dreze Jean. Universalisation with Quality and Equity. Economic and Political Weekly.

There is an urgent need for a simpler way to disburse funds. While the organizational structure and functions of the government should be decentralized, there is no need for funds to pass through the State, the District, the Block and the Village to the payees. Instead, the beneficiaries should get their funding directly. This shall be elaborated upon for each and every scheme. An alternate arrangement shall be presented at the end of this paper.

Schemes for Education of Girls and Women of Ministry of Human Resource Development (MHRD)

The Department of Elementary Education and Literacy is in charge of the MHRD's most ambitious schooling project—The Sarva Shiksha Abhiyan (SSA). The SSA serves as an umbrella scheme for schemes directly and indirectly beneficial to the girl child—the National Programme for the Education of Girls at an Elementary Level (NPEGEL) and the Early Childhood Care and Education (ECCE) Programme. The Education Guarantee Scheme under SSA also aims to provide vocational and non-formal education to out-of school children, of which, girls are intuitively significant in number. While these schemes have been designed, keeping in mind, groups like girls, SCs and STs who are often left out of the development process, the quality of schooling is a matter of concern. Other MHRD schemes include the Kasturba Gandhi Ballika Vidyalayas (KGBVs), the Mahila Samakhya Programme, the Mid-Day Meal Scheme and schemes for adult literacy.

A pattern that persists through the schemes of the Ministry of Human Resource Development is that they seek to reduce the costs of a girl's education, the opportunity cost of which is generally very high as a girl who is in school cannot do the housework and look after her siblings. Also they seek to increase the benefits of schooling. Thus it is likely that they might cause the benefits of educating a girl to outweigh the costs and ensure that she is sent to school.

An example is the Mid-Day Meal Scheme. It works as an additional benefit. The NPEGEL provides free uniforms and textbooks, which causes a reduction in the costs of schooling.

Moreover, the schemes also seek to set up Non-Formal Schools which provide bridge courses to mainstream out of school children, especially adolescent girls. Also, vocational training is provided.

Sarva Shiksha Abhiyan

The SSA was launched in accordance to the Eighty Sixth Constitutional Amendment for Universal Elementary Education (UEE) towards the end of the Ninth Five Year Plan in 2001 and was integrated with the District Primary Education Programme (DPEP). It was continued into the Tenth Five Year Plan. The aims and objectives of the SSA were rather ambitious. It was intended to ensure that all children were enrolled into the schooling system by 2003. All initially enrolled children were to complete five years of schooling by 2007 and eight years by 2010. By 2010, the SSA aimed to achieve universal retention.

The SSA was also an attempt to bridge gender and social disparities at the primary level by 2007 and at the elementary level by 2010. It was meant to improve access to education as well as the quality of elementary education. Areas of concern Needless to say, these ambitious objectives were not fulfilled. However, according to the Mid-Term Appraisal of the Tenth Five Year Plan, out of school children between the ages 6-14 were reduced from 42 million in 2002 to 8.1 million in 2004, which is rather dramatic. Though this figure has been accepted by the Planning Commission, the effectiveness of the SSA even with reference to initial enrolment is doubtful. Areas of concern regarding the SSA include poor teaching quality and infrastructure.

1. Poor teaching quality: By the government's own calculations, four out of ten children in government schools are likely to drop out before completing primary school.

According to Pratham's ASER Report in 2003, not more than 30 per cent of the school children in the age group 6-14 in an educationally well developed state like Maharashtra can read simple texts fluently or can solve simple arithmetic sums. Pratham also conducted a survey of 2500 children in 59 municipal wards in Patna. Out of these, 1000 were in government schools, 1000 were in private schools and 500 had not been enrolled at all. On a random check, the attendance was merely 40 per cent. 600 children who were in government schools weren't attending on the day of the check. Thus, it seems that in reality, 1100 children out of 2500 children were out of school. This was a more than significant 44 per cent. Less than half of the school-going children could read simple paragraphs or solve simple addition and subtraction sums.

2. Infrastructure

1. 0.18 million school buildings had been sanctioned, out of which, 0.117 million have been constructed as on 31 March 2007.
2. 0.69 million additional classrooms had been approved and merely 0.40 million were actually built.
3. 0.17 million drinking water facilities had been arranged for but only 0.14 million were actually provided.
4. 0.23 million toilets had been sanctioned of which 0.19 were constructed.
5. 1.012 million teachers were to be appointed but only 0.79 million were recruited in reality.

An Argument for Community Involvement

According to the Planning Commission in its Mid-Term Appraisal of the Tenth Five Year Plan in 2005, the Teacher's Education Programmes should have been merged with the SSA, Teaching and Learning Materials (TLM) should have been introduced and there was to be a greater involvement of local communities, Panchayati Raj Institutions and Non Government Organisations (NGOs) in order to check poor teaching quality and teacher absenteeism. Community involvement is usually a very good way to check teacher quality. Teachers should be hired by the School Management Committees rather than the State Government. The School Management Committees should comprise of parents and local authorities like Panchayati Raj Institutions. This will ensure that parents have a say in how well their children are educated. However, though the Panchayati Raj Institutions (PRI) has been established and though elections have been instituted and are taking place, PRIs have not been empowered enough through the effective transfer of functions, funds or functionaries. To encourage a greater role for the PRIs, the Planning Commission has recommended in its Mid-Term Appraisal, that a linkage should be introduced by means of which, release orders should be given to the States if and only if there is evidence that they have transferred functions, functionaries and financial resources to the PRIs. Also School Management Committees should be allowed these as well.

There are also various financial allegations against the SSA. The Indian Market Research Bureau records an instance of two districts in Jharkhand in which grants of Rs. 4.78 million were released to 2369 schools which did not exist other than on paper. In Gujarat, Rs. 0.4 million was diverted by the Gujarat Council of Educational Research and Training only to perform a Bhumipuja (a ritual that involves the worship of the land). There is also evidence on Teaching/ Learning Equipment Material Grants' inefficiencies. In Andhra Pradesh 7531 colour television sets were procured at a cost of Rs. 112.1 million for the upper primary section. It was found during the audit that these television sets were lying idle in at least 36 schools. This was because these schools did not have supplies of electricity in the first place.

In Uttar Pradesh as well, 51 out of 105 computers in 7 districts were lying dysfunctional due to lack of electricity. In Bihar, the reason for the non-utilisation of at least 247 computers was the inexistence of school buildings and the low availability of computer-trained teachers. This is another urgent reason for the integration of Teacher Education Programmes with the Sarva Shiksha Abhiyan.

Education Guarantee Scheme (EGS) or Schemes for Alternative and Innovative Education (AIE)

The EGS/AIE Schemes were launched under the SSA as successors to the Non-Formal Education Scheme launched in 1979 and revised in 1987. These targeted not only out-of-school children but also hardest-to-reach children *i.e.,* out of school girls, adolescent girls, school drop outs, children from habitations with no schools and working children. The target group was expected to comprise of children aged 6 to 14 and handicapped children aged 6 to 18. The EGS/AIE schemes covered 12 million people in 2003.

The objective of the scheme was to enroll children between 6 to 8 years of age into school. It was intended to arrange motivational courses to this end, if necessary. Children of ages 9 to 11 in non-formal schools were to be mainstreamed with the help of bridge courses and residential camps. Schools in school-less habitations were to be set up. Projects costing above Rs. 845 per child per annum for primary schools and above Rs. 1200 per child per annum would be approved by the Centre. Funding is done on a three tier system. EGS Centres and other State run Schools are funded on a 75:25 basis by the Centre and the States. Voluntary Agencies which run innovative schemes to enroll hardest-to-reach children into the schooling system are fully funded through Central grants.

The-Mid Term Appraisal of the Planning Commission recommended that EGS/AIE Centres should enroll the remaining 8.1 million out of school children (as of September

2004) and mainstream the 12 million children in formal schools. Details about programme implementation for 2006-7 are rather surprising. For one thing, Bihar and Jharkhand have done remarkably well. Bihar had a target of having 1.2 million children enrolled in EGS Centres. It succeeded in ensuring a current enrolment of 0.8 million, which is 70.33 per cent of the target. It also succeeded in setting up all the 15,423 EGS Centres that it had been targeting for 2006-07. Jharkhand succeeded in enrolling all the 0.7 million children and in setting up all the 17842 EGS Centres that it had been targeting. The Andaman and Nicobar Islands, Meghalaya, Mizoram, and Rajasthan met with similar success in meeting targets both in terms of number of children enrolled and number of EGS Centres set-up.

Assam exceeded its target when it came to current enrolment (0.39 million as opposed to a target of 0.35) but it met only (in contrast) 86.58 per cent of its target in terms of setting up EGS Centres. Either the rest of the centres weren't necessary or the student-teacher ratio has increased, in which case, there has possibly been a decline in the quality of education imparted. Himachal Pradesh fulfilled its target of setting up 2659 EGS Centres but it is still short of the 7979 children it had been trying to enroll.

In comparison, Punjab performed poorly. It met only 56.37 per cent of its target in setting up EGS Centres and 66.53 per cent of the current enrolment it had been aiming to achieve. The most inefficient performer was however, West Bengal. While it had established all the 19680 EGS Centres it had been aiming to, it had succeeded in enrolling merely 1.23 per cent (0.021 out of 1.7 million) of the children it had targeted. Once again, it is rather doubtful as to the quality of these EGS Centres and the attendance pattern of their students. The Social and Rural Research Institute, a branch of the Indian Market Research Bureau attests that Bihar, Uttar Pradesh, West Bengal Rajasthan, Jharkhand and Andhra Pradesh have the maximum number of out of school students. MHRD's data doesn't seem consistent with IMRB's results at all. IMRB claims that the schemes under the SSA have completely failed to reach their objectives. There were to be no out of school children in 2005. However, there were 13.6 million of them. According to the National Institute of Educational Planning and Administration the number of drop outs as a percentage of the total number of out-of school students—54.9 per cent was higher than the other 45.1 per cent which had never attended school. Out of 100 children enrolled in Class I, almost 63 were absent from mainstream education. Only 37 of these children reached Class X. The primary reasons for the high dropout rate were corporal punishment, boring and irrelevant curriculum and an inability to cope.

National Programme for Education of Girls at an Elementary Level (NPEGEL)

The National Programme for Education of Girls at an Elementary Level was started in September 2003 as an integral component of the Sarva Shiksha Abhiyan. It sought to distribute free textbooks for girls till Class VIII, construct separate toilets for girls and to conduct bridge camps for older out-of-school girls. The NPEGEL aimed at ensuring that 50 per cent of the newly recruited teachers were female and that learning materials would be gender sensitive. NPEGEL also intends to mobilize intensive community efforts and institute an innovation fund (for better enrolment and retention) per district.

As such, the NPEGEL provides additional provisions for enhancing the education of underprivileged/disadvantaged girls at an elementary level through more intense community mobilization, development of model schools in clusters and the provision of need based incentives like textbooks and uniforms. Concrete details of its implementation are, in fact, available. 29532 model schools or cluster schools (1 school for 8-10 villages) have been developed. 73788 teachers in educationally backward blocks have been sensitized to gender issues. 7713 additional rooms have been constructed in schools for space for teacher training and skill building for girls. Free uniforms have been distributed to 20 million girls in Educationally Backward Blocks. NPEGEL was expanded to 38748 clusters (8-10 villages) in 3122 blocks in 2006.

According to the mid-term appraisal of the Tenth Five Year Plan by the Planning Commission, areas of concern with respect to NPEGEL are factors leading to low learner's achievement including poor classroom transactions, lack of pupil evaluation and low proportion of female teachers. The Planning Commission recommends that the local community should be involved in monitoring school progress through Village Education Committees. The NPEGEL Scheme is essentially for the girl child only. The idea behind free textbooks and uniforms is to reduce the costs of schooling for the girl child. It is generally seen that when there are economic constraints, the girl child is the first of the children in a family, to be taken out of school. This is because the opportunity cost of educating a girl is generally high. In case of economic constraints, the daughter of the house must do the housework (as her mother must work) and various odd jobs (as a domestic servant for example). The sons are kept at school since they can be counted upon as a future investment while the girls are to be married off.

However, free uniforms and textbooks cannot be distributed forever. These are a temporary measure—a direct action rather than a policy action. The NPEGEL should focus on doing more than increasing enrolment. It should increase retention as well. NPEGEL should focus on more permanent facilities like the construction of girls' toilets and spreading awareness about the need for girls' education.

Mobilizing community organisations to maintain effective checks on teacher training exercises and service delivery is important. In Orissa, there has been an initiative in which

Mother Teresa Associations maintain a check on the attendance of teachers and children, the regularity of classes and the cleanliness of the school compound. Designated mothers are also required to bring out of school children in the neighbourhood by motivating parents. While NGOs and charity organisations can mobilize the community, the community itself can do a better job as it has more of an incentive to. The question is how will the government enable illiterate villagers, slum dwellers etcetera to come together, send their daughters to school and ensure that the benefits of schooling their daughters exceed the costs? To start with, there is a very low value attached to girls' education anyway. For this, the NPEGEL must spread awareness through publicity campaigns in addition to its other operations. Also, the schools that NPEGEL sets up should be exclusively for girls. Thus parents who are otherwise uncomfortable about sending their daughters to co-educational schools would have a school to send their daughters to.

Kasturbha Gandhi Balika Vidyalaya (KGBV)

Launched in July 2004, the KGBV sets up residential schools at the upper primary region-primarily for girls from SC, ST and OBC families as well as minority communities. The scheme is being implemented in Educationally Backward Blocks where the female rural literacy is below the national average. 75 per cent of the seats in KGBVs are reserved for SCs, STs, OBCs and minorities. The remaining 25 per cent of the vacancies are filled with girls of BPL families. The Government of India had sanctioned 1180 KGBVs as of 2006 but had made only 782 operational by September 2006. 52186 girls had been enrolled. The KGBV is being implemented in 24 States and 1 Union Territory. KGBV is as such, targeted at girls above ten years of age. Out of school girls of this age require bridge courses to mainstream them into KGBVs. In Karnataka, these are being provided in all the 58 KGBVs in operation in Educationally Backward Blocks, in co-ordination with the Ministry of Women and Child Development, Mahila Samakhya Officials and NGOs. Madhya Pradesh offers two types of bridge courses—non residential and residential. Non Residential Bridge courses are offered in areas in which there are a substantial number of out of school children (10 or more). Residential courses are offered only in tribal areas. Out of the 959 residential bridge courses offered, 671 are for girls and 39201 girls have been enrolled in bridge courses in Madhya Pradesh.

From instances of implementation in Karnataka, it can be seen that KGBV has much scope for participation. 27 out of the 58 KGBVs run in Karnataka are run by Mahila Sanghas (Women's groups formed under the Mahila Samakhya Scheme. However, to ensure proper service delivery in terms of free uniforms, textbooks and mid-day meals, more active participation is required. Like EGS Centres, KGBVs too, should be run by School Management Committees consisting of members of the Panchayat, Local Government authorities, Mahila Sangha women and more importantly, of parents and teachers.

Early Childhood Care and Education (ECCE)

The ECCE was an optional component of the District Primary Education Programme while it was still in operation. Currently, the ECCE is still being carried out, though in a small way, under the Sarva Shiksha Abhiyan. The ECCE aims at setting up pre-schools to prepare children for schooling. It has an indirect bearing on education for girls as with her siblings in school, the girl child need not assume sibling care responsibilities during school hours and can therefore, attend school. ECCE is run with innovation funds from the MHRD through School Management Committees, Village Education Committees and Education Guarantee Centres. To avoid duplication of efforts, ECCE Centres are instituted in areas with no Integrated Child Development Services Centres for pre-school children run by the Ministry of Women and Child Development.

However, according to the Planning Commission in 2005, there aren't enough ECCE or ICDS Centres. ECCE should include provisions for training teachers on a need basis and for play-way kits for innovative teaching.

Recommendations

It is important to remember that the girl child is most susceptible to low school quality, low teaching quality and lack of innovative ways of learning. Thanks to the high opportunity cost of schooling a girl child and because educating a girl is like "watering someone else's courtyard" (as she will get married and not be a part of her parents' family any longer), if a girl fails a class or two, she is very likely to be forced to drop out. Thus, while the NPEGEL and EGS schemes may cause a girl child to get enrolled into school, they are not likely to ensure that she will not drop out. For this, a two pronged strategy is important.

1. Start a massive publicity campaign extolling the virtues of educating a girl and the benefit that might accrue to her family in the form of monetary gain once she starts earning and status and prestige in the community. Education is sensitive to interpersonal motivation. If one family sends its girls to school, its neighbours are likely to do so as well. The publicity should also invite parents to form associations and register with the district authorities. They should be informed of the benefits of organising themselves to protest against the low teaching standards and to ensure teacher regularity and service delivery.
2. The Centre should release its grants for the next year of the scheme if and only if there is evidence of community mobilization. This should imply the

formation of women's Self-Help Groups, Parent Teacher Associations and School Management Committees. These can be trained by NGOs hired by the State governments or district authorities to insist upon checking records for teachers' attendance and regularity.

These associations can be a very effective check upon inefficiencies related to teaching learning materials as well. They will ensure that all television sets and computers are in operation.

Only local groups like women's associations, School Managing Committees and Parent Teacher Associations have the incentive to maintain checks upon how well the children of the community are being educated. While they may pay low fees to government schools, they incur huge opportunity costs in the form of their children's time. Thus it is the beneficiaries of the schemes—the parents and the students who should be empowered enough to ensure service delivery under the Sarva Shiksha Abhiyan. Perhaps the CAS should fund School Management Committees directly once they are formed by district authorities or on their own initiative. This will empower local bodies as they will get more funds than they would have gotten had it trickled through the state and district channels. With these funds, the SMCs can ensure the construction of schooling infrastructure and the provision of Teaching and Learning Materials. The SMC should be able to hire, pay and fire the school teachers.

The ECCE should also ensure crèches in the proximity of each and every coeducational and girls' school-primary as well as secondary. This would enable the elder daughters of households to leave their younger siblings in the care of trained personnel. (Community organisations should see to it that personnel in ECCE crèches and pre-schools are trained.)

Mahila Samakhya (MS) Programme

Launched in 1988 in accordance to the New Education Policy of 1986, the Mahila Samakhya Programme seeks to benefit women of all ages, especially those from socially and economically marginalized groups. It aims to integrate formal and non-formal education for girls, education schemes for adult women and vocational training for girls and women.

Launched as a pilot project in 10 districts in Uttar Pradesh, Gujarat and Karnataka in 1988, the Mahila Samakhya Scheme covered 9000 villages in 60 backward districts in 10 States—Andhra Pradesh, Assam, Bihar, Jharkhand, Karnataka, Kerala, Gujarat and Uttar Pradesh as of 2000. 0.2 million women had been actively mobilized. Its nodal agencies are voluntary organisations, women's associations and NGOs, all of which are eligible for Central grants. These agencies set-up Mahila Samakhya Societies or Mahila Sanghas to take-up field projects for empowerment and education and to develop means of learning and instruction.

The predominant composition of the Mahila Sanghas is SC/ST women belonging to landless and marginalized families engaged in wage labour. Bringing these women into Sanghas makes them active agents in their own and other women's empowerment. The idea behind founding Mahila Sanghas was to enable women to affirm their potential and to move from situations of passive acceptance to assertion and collective action. The Mahila Samakhya Scheme was to create independent collectives of women to initiate and sustain social change.

One of its more well-defined aims was to consciencitise adult women to take familial decisions in favour of their daughters' education. (As aforementioned, the regression co-efficient between the presence of an educated mother and the initial enrolment of the girl child tested positive and significant as per the results of the PROBE Survey by Dreze and Kingdon.) The Mahila Samakhya Scheme empowered adult women to take decisions regarding the family. It was expected that empowered mothers would want to educate their daughters. In fact the Mahila Samakhya Scheme is also called The Education for Women's Equality Scheme. This is due to the various innovation projects taken up by Mahila Sanghas to educate their daughters. One of these is the concept of the Mahila Shiksha Kendra – a residential learning centre facilitating the emergence of alternative forums for women like women's courts and health centres. The Mahila Shiksha Kendra is an innovative women centered educational facility for women in rural areas. In Andhra Pradesh, two women from the Sangha act as wardens in the Mahila Shiksha Kendra and cook for the girls. A gender training manual for Non-Formal Educational instructors was developed on the initiative of a Sangha in Karnataka. Mahila Samakhya: A Success?

For most women, organising themselves and attending meetings was an experience in itself. A Sangha woman from Tehri in Uttar Pradesh reported being told by her husband to stay at home and finish the housework instead of going out and 'gossiping' with the Mahila Sangha. If meetings delayed her cooking, she was beaten. Women in Andhra Pradesh were told "Today you could not cook because of the meeting; tomorrow you will ask men to wash clothes. What do you think you are going to do? Rule the country?" The Mahila Samakhya Scheme also caused women to be seen and noticed in areas erstwhile reserved for men, primarily high caste men. The Mahila Samakhya Scheme has numerous success stories.

1. In the Attanoor Village in Raichur, an all women panchayat confronted land grabbers who were illegally using one and a half acres of common land, confiscated it and used it for the construction of community toilets.
2. Pushpalata, a ward member of the panchayat in Ryalapalli village, Gangadhara Mandal, Karimnagar district in 2000 confronted the Sarpanch about how

he had spent the money obtained by the panchayat for the auction of two tamarind trees. When she was told that he had spent it on valves for the irrigation system, she was able to prove that the State Government had provided the valves free of cost. The money was returned.

3. In Sitapur in Uttar Pradesh, the Mahila Sangha was able to change a custom in which a female doll was beaten to shreds in public on Nag Panchami to one in which it is rocked upon a swing. This had a powerful symbolic significance. A parallel custom was one in which brides were beaten with sticks once they entered their marital home. The Mahila Sangha changed this into one in which they are offered sweets.

However, these are isolated incidences. It can easily be seen that the short-term goals of the Mahila Samakhya Scheme have barely been defined at all. Success stories have happened but these are not universal—they are merely inspirational stories about the achievements of a few Sangha women—not those of the scheme itself. The failure of the Mahila Samakhya Scheme lies in its poor and complex organization.

Organizational Structure

The Mahila Samakhya Programme is implemented through autonomous registered societies at the state level. These are sponsored by the Centre through a complex organizational structure that involves a State Programme Office and a District Implementation Unit which forms a Federation of Mahila Sanghas. The body that is actually responsible for the implementation of the Mahila Samakhya Scheme is the MS Block Resource Unit which works under the supervision of the Federation. A woman facilitator known as a Sahyogini is responsible to the Mahila Sangha for every cluster of 10 villages. The State MS Society Executive Committee

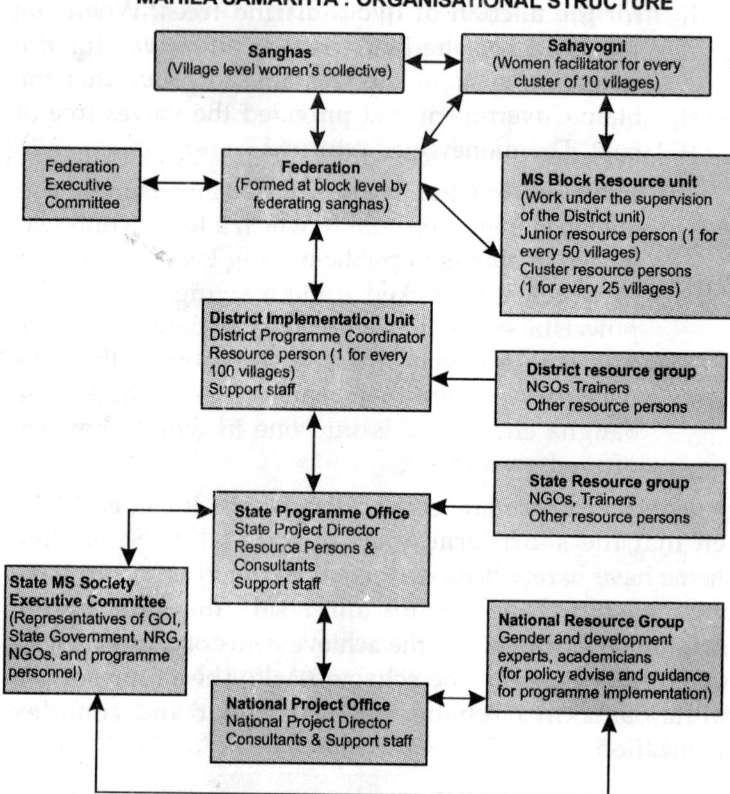

Source: MHRD. Mahila Samakhya Organizational Structure. Accessed on 13 June 2007 at www.education.nic.in///MS/MSorganogram.pdf

comprises of the representatives of the Government of India, National Resource Group (Gender and development expert academicians), NGOs and programme personnel.

The MHRD reports that in Gujarat, the State Programme Office hardly functions due to frequent changes in leadership and management inefficiencies. It affords poor research and documentation support to district implementation units. There is no systematic approach for staff planning, recruitment, training, capability development and retention, assessment and discontinuation. Funds from the Government of India are almost never available within the stipulated time frame. MHRD suspects gross financial irregularities in the districts' and state offices and ad holism in purchases due to the non existence of a committee for purchases and due to the lack of stringent measures. What is true of Gujarat is possibly true of each and every state. The MHRD does not have as detailed an evaluation of other States and is thus unable to state so for sure. Nonetheless, incentives for corruption and inefficiency clearly exist.

Recommendations

1. To start with, the objectives of the scheme must be clearly defined. The Mahila Samakhya Scheme has no clear aims. The creation of Mahila Shiksha Kendra's through the formation of a women's association should be its focus.

2. Data on the number of Mahila Shiksha Kendra's in each state is essential. It should be published on the MHRD site.

3. Block and District Authorities should launch publicity campaigns adjuring women to organise themselves into Sanghas. NGOs and Women's groups should actively persuade women to form associations at the grassroots level. These institutions should be directly funded by the Centre. They should register themselves with the State which must transmit the list of Block and District Authorities, NGOs and women's groups working towards making the scheme a success, and the grants they need, to the MHRD for funding and monitoring purposes.

4. Every Mahila Sangha, whether formed by NGOs and women's groups, formed voluntarily, or formed by Block or District authorities, should be registered with the District authorities. It should get its funds directly from the Centre. Funds for the next year of implementation should not be provided unless there is evidence of the establishment of at least one Mahila Shiksha Kendra.

5. Every Mahila Sangha must be trained in reading, writing, accountancy and the use of the Right to Information Act by trainers recruited by District Authorities.

6. Mahila Sanghas should constitute a part of the School Management Committees run under the Sarva Shiksha Abhiyan and they should see to it that girls' toilets, classrooms etcetera are functional and in good condition. They should supervise gender sensitizing activities for teachers under NPEGEL and they should ensure teacher regularity.

The trouble with the Mahila Samakhya Scheme is that all the existing literature available on it cites instances of success and much rhetoric. It is true that the concept of women working for their own education and equality is a splendid idea but the way in which it has been carried out since the late 1980's is not very organized. It has been under the DPEP in states like Bihar. However, if it has to be a separate scheme, it has to have its own structure. (Else it should be merged with the SSA.) The prevalent structure is much too complex and ineffective. Even MHRD reports corruption at the Block and District levels in Gujarat. Funds are never available within the stipulated time period. The State Project Offices are far too weak to support the Block and District officials with supervision, research and co-ordination. Instead, the various institutions and the Sanghas must be paid directly by the Centre. Funding should be centralized though supervision, monitoring, publicity and training should be the responsibility of Block and District Authorities.

The Mid-Day Meal (MDM) Scheme

According to the afore-mentioned PROBE Survey, the presence of Mid-Day Meals in the villages increased the probability that a girl child would be enrolled in a school by 15 per cent. The MDM has this effect as it increases the benefit of schooling a girl as perceived by her parents. (A girl generally has a higher opportunity cost of schooling as she is expected to look after the household, especially if her mother is working. So an increased benefit will swing the implicit cost-benefit analysis in a parent's mind in favour of schooling the girl child.) The MDM also reduces caste biases as it forces children of all castes to eat together. 100g of food grain per child per school day is distributed to all children in government schools. MDM is also known as the Nutritional Support to Primary Education Scheme.

When it comes to the Mid-Day Meal Scheme however, there are huge areas of concern. To start with there are large inter-state variations. Karnataka's centralized cooking and delivery of cooked food to various schools is replicable in other States as well. It has been found to be rather efficient in terms of costs and time. Self-Help Groups and NGOs are providing cooked food to school going children in Andhra Pradesh, Karnataka, Orissa and Uttar Pradesh. The MHRD reports the provision of mid-day meals to approximately 1120 million children in 2005. However, enquiries at a colony in Dakshinpuri, Delhi and a meeting with a member of the office staff of a government school revealed that Mid-Day meals were being provided only at Sarvodaya schools. (For a statewide list of the number of primary schools and EGS/ AIE Centres in which the scheme is in operation, see Annexure 2.)

The Planning Commission suggests that a concurrent evaluation of the Mid-Day Meal Scheme should be launched in all states. State Governments should make arrangements for Public-Private Partnerships, social audit and greater accountability.

Recommendations

The Mid-Day Meal Scheme must be universalized. It should be subject to a social audit in all states and it should definitely be provided in all government schools (not just Sarvodaya Vidyalayas) – both formal and non-formal, particularly in girls' schools and even in secondary schools. The trouble with the Mid-Day Meal Scheme is that it is, once again a direct action rather than a policy action. It may address both enrolment and retention but it does not help the provision of an education of quality. Students may enroll themselves just for the meal and may not attend class. This should be actively checked and students should be allowed their meal if and only if they have attended their classes.

The State Government should outsource the delivery of the mid-day meal to local bodies comprising of parents, teachers and local officials like members of the panchayat. They could recruit private contractors to cook and deliver the meals.

The Education Schemes of the Ministry of Women and Child Development

The Department of Women and Child Development had been established in 1985 under the Ministry of Human Resource Development. However, it had been constituted into a separate Ministry on 30 October 2006. Since then, it has continued funding and designing several schemes-primarily the Balika Samriddhi Yojana, the Integrated Child Development Services and the Kishori Shakti Yojana. At this juncture, it is essential to mention that the MWCD should set up an information facilitation centre for the convenience of RTI applicants. It was almost impossible to file RTIs. The Public Information Officer was "at a meeting".

Balika Samriddhi Yojana

The Balika Samriddhi Yojana was started on 2 October, 1997 and was revised in 1999. It targets BPL girls and daughters of rag pickers, vegetable/fish sellers, pavement dwellers and the like. Those who wish to avail of the benefit from this scheme must apply to Anganwadi workers (who work in pre-schooling, health and supplementary nutrition centres for an honorarium), auxiliary nurses, midwives, revenue village accountants, school teachers and panchayat/municipal staff who are to collect applications. Under this Scheme, the State deposits Rs. 500 in an interest bearing account in the name of the girl child. When the girl turns eighteen, she may avail of the money if she is still unmarried (as certified by the Gram Panchayat). Annual scholarships are also awarded under this Scheme. These are incremental in order to encourage retention.

The money in this account can be withdrawn with sanction from the mother/guardian of the girl child only for premium payments under the Bhagyashree Balika Kalyan Bima Yojana and to pay for textbooks and uniforms. So far, the scheme has benefited 3.15 million girls born on or after 15 August 1997. The girls are to reach class X in 2012. No State Government has reported insuring any of the girls under the Bhagyashree Balika Kalyan Bima Yojana. As per the decision of Planning Commission, the Balika Samriddhi Yojana is soon to be transferred to the State Sector.

Recommendations

To evaluate the Balika Samridhi Yojana, more data on the implementation is necessary. The scheme shows an element of sensitivity to the incremental opportunity cost of the education of a girl child. The number of beneficiaries is fairly impressive. However, the MWCD should insist on States insuring the girls under the Bhagyashree Balika Kalyan Bima Yojana. Also, girls should be enrolled in schools in which textbooks and uniforms are free. Moreover, there should be specific centres in which families can apply for benefits under the BSY Scheme. The annual budgetary outlay for the scheme should be decided on the basis of the number of applicants.

Integrated Child Development Services (ICDS)

The ICDS seeks to promote preschool education and to train 'Anganwadi' workers, primary school teachers and health workers to benefit children between 0 to 6 years of age, pregnant women and nursing mothers from the poorest of poor families, disadvantaged areas, backward and rural areas, tribal areas and slums. Activities under the ICDS include the provision of supplementary nutrition, referral services, nutrition and health education, preschool education, immunization and health checkups. ICDS also aims to provide a foundation for the proper psychological development of children.

The ICDS is an integrated approach for converging basic services through community based Anganwadi workers and helpers, supportive community structures and women's groups. In addition to providing preschool education, supplementary nutrition and health care, an Anganwadi worker is expected to maintain statistics on birth and deaths, keep records of supplies of food and educational material and to list women eligible to access doles and stipends under various schemes. However, she is not even entitled to the minimum wage. Nor is she rendered professional training as such. 32.1 million women and children have benefited from the ICDS as against a target of 27.7 million as per the Planning Commission's Mid-Term Appraisal of the Tenth Five Year Plan. The Planning Commission, however, notes that the number of crèches (12470) has not risen since 1993. It believes that crèche services should be integrated with ICDS. This is because pre-school education must be focused upon to keep girls in school (in case sibling care responsibilities keep older girls at home). SCERT (State Councils for Educational Research and Training) should train the Anganwadi workers to meet this critical requirement of preschool education.

Areas of Concern

The trouble with the ICDS however, is that it has not been universalized. According to Jean Dreze, there are legal, political and social reasons for the universalisation of the ICDS. To start with, the Supreme Court had declared on 28 November 2001 that the Government should ensure a functional anganwadi centre in every settlement. ICDS should be extended to all children under the age of six. This is necessary not only to ensure that adolescent girls go to school but also to provide nutrition and healthcare to children under six and to prepare them for school. The political argument deals with the United Progressive Alliance government's promises under the Common Minimum Programme. The social argument is most compelling—ICDS provides more equal opportunities for growth and development in early childhood. There are also various other quality constraints. In Bihar, 85 per cent of the supervisory posts under ICDS were found to be vacant. 18 per cent of ICDS projects in the state had no supervisors at all. In Jharkhand, the post of Child Development Project Officer was vacant in approximately half of the projects. On a statewide analysis on the basis of the FOCUS (Focus on Children Under Six) Index, Tamil Nadu fared better than Maharashtra, Uttar Pradesh and the North Indian States—Chhattisgarh, Himachal Pradesh, Rajasthan and Uttar Pradesh combined for most indicators. It had the lowest number of Anganwadi Centres in which the overall functioning was rated as 'poor' by the Survey Team. In Tamil Nadu, the motivation of mothers to send their children to school was the highest. Uttar Pradesh on the other hand, fared miserably. It had the highest number of Anganwadi Centres in which the survey team declared the overall functioning as 'poor' and the lowest proportion of villages in which mothers were motivated to send their children to school.

Dreze partly attributes the success of the ICDS in Tamil Nadu to women's agency. In Tamil Nadu, the ICDS was managed almost entirely by women and not just at the Anganwadi level. The women of the community had an incentive to run the ICDS well. They wanted to ensure their children's health and pre-schooling. Meanwhile, mothers could go to work and elder sisters could go to school. Thus, women helped to hold the system accountable and to make health and nutrition into political issues.

Kishori Shakti Yojana (KSY)

The Kishori Shakti Yojana is a redesign of the Adolescent Girls' Scheme which was under the ICDS. Like its precedent scheme, the KSY seeks to benefit girls of 11 to 18 years of age. Its objectives involve improving the nutritional, health and development status of adolescent girls, promoting awareness of health, hygiene, nutrition and family care, sending out of school girls back to school through bridge courses and non-formal education channels as well as imparting vocational training and sex education.

It differs from the Adolescent Girls Scheme as it has an extended coverage of the earlier scheme, significant content enrichment and a strengthened training component. 6118 blocks have been covered under this scheme. It also functions through Anganwadi Working Centres.

Recommendations

1. More crèche services need to be offered to increase girls' enrolment by relieving them temporarily of sibling care responsibilities.

2. Anganwadi workers need to be paid a higher honorarium.

3. The MWCD should not release the grants for the next year to the State without sufficient evidence of training programmes to Anganwadi workers and helpers through NGOs dealing with health and pre-school education.

4. In areas in which the Mahila Samakhya Scheme is in operation, Mahila Sanghas should operate the ICDS Centres.

5. The MWCD should not release grants to the State Government without sufficient evidence of an Anganwadi Centre in every settlement. The State Governments should provide reports of the number of settlements and on whether each has an ICDS centre. NGOs and social workers should file applications under the Right to Information to ensure that this has been done.

Looking Ahead

What contributes to the inefficiency of the Centrally Sponsored Schemes with regard to quality of education provided is the lack of local participation. State Governments, Block and District Authorities cannot ensure that these schemes function smoothly. The targeted beneficiaries should be empowered to ensure proper service delivery. This can be done through massive publicity campaigns to exhort parents, teachers and women etcetera to get together, organise and register them with the District Authorities. The Block Authorities and Panchayats should also persuade beneficiaries to form Self-Help Groups. Once these Self-Help Groups, School Management Committees and Mahila Sanghas are formed, they should be funded directly from the Central Accounting System set up by the RBI, on a release order from the concerned Ministry in the Government of India once it receives a list of all the Committees. This will save inefficiencies in the trickle down of funds from the Centre to the State to the District to the Block Authorities, in which case funds might be 'parked' or simply, siphoned away.

While measures like free uniforms and textbooks are effective in raising enrolment, they may not increase retention. For the latter, there should be a greater focus on proper service delivery and on the quality of infrastructure and teaching. Lastly, research institutes should run social audits on all these schemes and should evaluate and criticize them regularly. The Right to Information Act should be used constantly by Social Service Activists and Feminists to seek data on ground implementation.

CHAPTER

6

Literacy and Employment in India

Literacy in India is key for socio-economic progress, and the Indian *literacy rate* grew to 66 per cent in 2007 from 12 per cent at the end of *British rule* in 1947. Although this was a greater than fivefold improvement, the level is well below the world average literacy rate of 84 per cent, and India currently has the largest *illiterate* population of any nation on earth. Despite government programmes, India's literacy rate increased only "sluggishly," and a 1990 study estimated that it would take until 2060 for India to achieve universal literacy at then—current rate of progress. The 2001 census, however, indicated a 1991-2001 decadal literacy growth of 12.63 per cent, which is the fastest-ever on record.

There is a wide gender disparity in the literacy rate in India: adult (15+ years) literacy rates in 2009 were 76.9 per cent for men and 54.5 per cent for women. The low female literacy rate has had a dramatically negative impact on *family planning and population stabilization efforts* in India. Studies have indicated that female literacy is a strong predictor of the use of contraception among married Indian couples, even when women do not otherwise have economic independence. The 2001 census provided a positive indication that growth in female literacy rates (14.38%) was substantially faster than in male literacy rates (11.13%) in the 1991-2001 decadal period, which means the gender gap appears to be narrowing.

Comparative Literacy Statistics

About 35 per cent of world's illiterate population is Indian and, based on historic patterns of literacy growth across the world, India may account for a majority of the world's illiterates by 2020. The Table below shows the adult and youth literacy rates for India and some neighbouring countries in 2002. Adult literacy rate is based on the 15+ years age group, while Youth literacy rate is for the 15–24 years age group (*i.e.*, youth is a subset of adults).

Table 6.1

Country	Adult Literacy Rate	Youth Literacy Rate
China	93.3% (2007)[14]	98.9% (2004)[15]
Sri Lanka	90.8 (2007)	98.0
Burma	89.9% (2007)[16]	94.4% (2004)[17]
Iran	82.4% (2007)[18]	95% (2002)[19]
World Average	84% (1998)[4]	88% (2001)[20]
India	**66.0% (2007)[3]**	**82% (2001)[3]**
Nepal	56.5 (2007)	62.7
Pakistan	54.2 (2007([21]	53.9
Bangaldesh	53.5 (2007)	49.7

Growth of Literacy

Literacy in India grew very slowly until independence in 1947. An acceleration in the rate of literacy growth occurred in the 1991-2001 period. During the British period, progress of education was rather tardy. Between 1881-82 and 1946-47, the number of primary schools grew from 82,916 to 134,866 and the number of students grew from 2,061,541 to 10,525,943. Literacy rates in British India rose from 3.2 per cent in 1881 to 7.2 per cent in 1931 and 12.2 per cent in 1947. In 2000-01, there were 60,840 pre-primary and pre-basic schools, and 664,041 primary and junior basic schools. Total enrollment at the primary level has increased from 19,200,000 in 1950-51 to 109,800,000 in 2001-02. The number of high schools in 2000-01 was higher than the number of primary schools at the time of independence.

In 1944, the Government of British India presented a plan, called the *Sergeant Scheme* for the educational reconstruction of India, with a goal of producing 100 per cent literacy in the country within 40 years, *i.e.,* by 1984. Although the 40 year time-frame was derided at the time by leaders of the *Indian independence movement* as being too long a period to achieve universal literacy, India had only just crossed the 64 per cent level by the 2001 census.

Post Independence

The provision of universal and compulsory education for all children in the age group of 6-14 was a cherished national ideal and had been given overriding priority by incorporation as a *Directive Policy in Article 45 of the Constitution,* but it is still to be achieved more than half a century since the Constitution was adopted in 1949. *Parliament* has passed the Constitution 86th Amendment Act, 2002, to make elementary education a *Fundamental Right* for children in the age group of 6–14 years. In order to provide more funds for education, an education cuss of 2 per cent has been imposed on all direct and indirect central taxes through the Finance (No.2) Act, 2004. Since independence, the literacy rate grew from 18.33 per cent in 1951, to 28.30 per cent in 1961, 34.45 per cent in 1971, 43.57 per cent in 1981, 52.21 per cent in 1991, and 64.84 per cent in 2001. During the same period, the population grew from 361 million to 1,028 million.

Literacy Rate Variations between States

Kerala is the most literate state in India, with 90.92 per cent literacy, followed closely by *Mizoram* at 88.80 per cent. *Bihar* is the least literate state in India with 47 per cent literacy. Several other social indicators of the two states are correlated with these rates, such as life expectancy at birth (71.61 for males and 75 for females in Kerala, 65.66 for males and 64.79 for females in Bihar), infant mortality per 1,000 live births (10 in Kerala, 61 in Bihar), birth rate per 1,000 people (16.9 in Kerala, 30.9 in Bihar) and death rate per 1,000 people (6.4 in Kerala, 7.9 in Bihar). *Ernakulum* district in Kerala was the first district to reach the 100 per cent literacy level in India. Every census since 1881 had indicated rising literacy in the country, but the population growth rate had been high enough that the absolute number of illiterates rose with every decade. The 1991-2001 decade is the first census period when the absolute number of Indian illiterates declined (by 32 million), indicating that the literacy growth rate is now outstripping the population growth rate. Bihar, *Nagaland* and *Manipur* were the only states in the 1991-2001 period where the absolute number of illiterates rose, although even there the percentage of illiterates fell.

Bihar was the only remaining Indian state in the 2001 census where the majority of the population (53%) was illiterate. It was also the only state where less than 60 per cent of the male population was literate. Six Indian states account for about 70 per cent of all illiterates in India: *Uttar Pradesh, Bihar, Madhya Pradesh, Rajasthan, Andhra Pradesh* and *West Bengal*. Slightly less than half of all Indian illiterates (48.12%) are in the six Hindi-speaking states of Uttar Pradesh, Bihar, Rajasthan, Madhya Pradesh, Jharkhand and Chhattisgarh. Large variations in literacy exist even between contiguous states. While there are a few states at the top and bottom, most states are just above or below the national average.

Learning's from State Literacy Efforts in India

Several states in India have executed successful programmes to boost literacy rates. Over time, a set of factors have emerged as being key to success: official will to succeed, deliberate steps to engage the community in administering the programme, adequate funding for infrastructure and teachers, and provisioning additional services which are considered valuable by the community (such as free school lunches).

Bihar Literacy Challenges

Bihar has the lowest literacy rate in India and, in the 2001 census, was the only Indian state where the majority of the population (53%) was illiterate. Even in Bihar, however, the literacy rate is rising: from 39 per cent in 1991 to 47 per cent in 2001. The Government of Bihar has launched several programmes to boost literacy, and its Department of Adult Education even won a UNESCO award in 1981.

Extensive impoverishment, entrenched hierarchical social divisions and the lack of correlation between educational attainment and job opportunities are often cited in studies of the hurdles literacy programmes face in Bihar. Children from "lower castes" are frequently denied school attendance and harassed when they do attend. In areas where there is no discrimination, poor funding and impoverished families means that children often cannot afford textbooks and stationery. When children do get educated, the general lack of economic progress in the state means that government jobs are the only alternative to farm labour, yet these jobs, in practice, require bribes to secure—which poorer families cannot afford. This leads to educated youths working on the farms, much as uneducated ones do, and leads parents to question the investment of sending children to school in the first place. Bihar's government schools have also faced teacher absenteeism, leading the state government to threaten withholding of salaries of teachers who failed to conduct classes on a regular basis. To incentivize students to attend, the government announced a Rupee 1 per schooldays grant to poor children who show-up to school.

Kerala Literacy Successes

Kerala undertook a "*campaign for total literacy* in *Ernakulum* district in the late 1980s," with a "*fusion between the district administration headed by its Collector on one side and, on the other side, voluntary groups, social activists and others."* On February 4, 1990, Ernakulum was certified as being 100% literate. The Government of Kerala then replicated the initiative on a statewide level, launching the Kerala State Literacy Campaign. First, households were surveyed with door-to-door, multistage survey visits to form an accurate picture of the literacy landscape and areas that needed special focus. Then, *Kala Jathas* (cultural troupes) and *Saksharta Pad Yatras* (Literacy Foot Marches) were organized to generate awareness of the campaign and create a receptive social atmosphere for the programme. An integrated management system was created involving state officials, prominent social figures, local officials and senior voluntary workers to oversee the execution of the campaign.

Himachal Pradesh Literacy Successes

Strong government action and community support made *Himachal Pradesh* one of India's most literate states by 2001 Himachal Pradesh underwent a "Schooling Revolution" in the 1961-2001 period that has been called *"even more impressive than Kerala's."* Kerala has led the nation in literacy rates since the 19th century and seen sustained initiatives for over 150 years, whereas Himachal Pradesh's literacy rates in 1961 were below the national average in every age group. In the three decadal 1961-1991 period, female literacy in the 15–19 years age group went from 11 per cent to 86 per cent. School attendance for both boys and girls in the 6-14 year age group stood at over 97 per cent each when measured in the 1998-99 school year. A key factor that has been credited for these advances is Himachal's cultural background. Himachal Pradesh is a *Himalayan* state with lower social stratification than many other states, which enables social programmes to be carried out more smoothly. Once the Government of Himachal Pradesh was able to establish a social norm that *"schooling is an essential part of every child's upbringing,"* literacy as a normal attribute of life was adopted very rapidly. Government efforts in expanding schools and providing teachers were sustained after the 1960s and communities often responded very collaboratively, including with constructing school rooms and providing firewood essential during the Himalayan winters.

Mizoram Literacy Successes

Mizoram's literacy rate rose rapidly after independence: from 31.14 per cent in 1951 to 88.80 per cent in 2001. As in Himachal Pradesh, Mizoram has a social structure that is relatively free of hierarchy and strong official intent to produce total literacy. The government identified illiterates and organized an administrative structure that engaged officials and community leaders, and manned by "animators" who were responsible for teaching five illiterates each. Mizoram established 360 continuing education centers to handle continued education beyond the initial literacy teaching and to provide an educational safety net for school dropouts.

Tamil Nadu Literacy Successes

Tamil Nadu is the most literate state of India according to the HRD ministry of India's 2003 statistics. Starting in 1982, Tamil Nadu took an approach to promoting literacy based on free lunches for schoolchildren, *"ignoring cynics who said it was an electoral gimmick and economists who said it made little fiscal sense."* The then Chief Minister of Tamil Nadu, M. G. Ramachandran launched the programme, which resembled a similar initiative in 19th century *Japan*, because *"he had experienced as a child what it was like to go hungry to school with the family having no money to buy food"*. Eventually, the programme covered all children under the age of 15, as well as pregnant women for the first four months of their pregnancy. Tamil Nadu's literacy rate rose from 54.4 per cent in 1981 to 73.4 per cent in 2001. In 2001, the *Supreme Court of India* instructed all state governments to implement free school lunches in all government-funded schools, but implementation has been patchy due to corruption and social issues. Despite these hurdles, 120 million receive free lunches in Indian schools every day, making it the largest school meal programme in the world.

Rajasthan Literacy Successes

Rajasthan had the biggest percentage decadal (1991-2001) increase in literacy of all Indian states, from about 38 per cent to about 61 per cent, a leapfrog that has been termed "spectacular" by some observers. Aggressive state government action, in the form of the *District Primary Education Programme,* the *Shiksha Karmi* initiative and the *Lok Jumbish* programme, are credited with the rapid improvement. Virtually every village in Rajasthan now has primary school coverage. When statehood was granted to Rajasthan in 1956, it was the least literate state in India with a literacy rate of 18 per cent.

Social Commentary

In his essay on *Social Infrastructure As Important As Physical Infrastructure* published in *India Development Report 2002,* Kirit S. Parikh had pointed out, "With a literacy rate of 65, we have 296 million illiterates, age seven years and above, as per the 2001 census. The number of illiterates today exceeds the population of the country of around 270 million at Independence, age seven and above."

In his book *The Argumentative Indian, Amartya Sen* notes, on the basis of investigations by Pratichi Trust, set-up with the proceeds of his Nobel award, carried out in West Bengal and Jharkhand, that absenteeism of comparatively well-paid teachers, particularly where bulk of the students come from scheduled castes and tribes, poses a major problem. Students are circumstantially forced to go in for private tuitions. He concludes, "Sometimes the very institutions that were created to overcome disparities and barriers have tended to act as reactionary influences in reinforcing inequality… The teachers' unions, which have a very positive role to play in protecting the interests of teachers and have played that part well in the past, are often are turning into an influence that reinforces the neglect of the interests of children from desperately underprivileged families. There is evidence of hardening of class barriers that separate the newly affluent teachers from the impoverished rural poor."

Literacy Efforts

The *right to education* is a fundamental *human right*, and UNESCO aims at education for all by 2015. India, along with the Arab states and sub-Saharan Africa, has a literacy level below the threshold level of 75 per cent, but efforts are on to achieve that level. The campaign to achieve at least the threshold literacy level represents the largest ever civil and military mobilization in the country. *International Literacy Day* is celebrated each year on 8 September with the aim to highlight the importance of literacy to individuals, communities and societies.

National Literacy Mission

The *National Literacy Mission*, launched in 1988, aimed at attaining a literacy rate of 75 per cent by 2007. It imparts functional literacy to non-literates in the age group of 15–35 years. The *Total Literacy Campaign* is the principal strategy of the NLM for eradication of illiteracy. The *Continuing Education Scheme* provides a learning continuum to the efforts of the Total Literacy and *Post literacy* programmes.

Sarva Siksha Abhiyan

The *Sarva Siksha Abhiyan* (*Hindi* for *Total Literacy Campaign*) was launched in 2001 to ensure that all children in the 6–14 year age-group attend school and complete eight years of schooling by 2010. An important component of the scheme is the *Education Guarantee Scheme and Alternative and Innovative Education*, meant primarily for children in areas with no formal school within a one kilometre radius. The centrally sponsored

District Primary Education Programme, launched in 1994, had opened more than 160,000 new schools by 2005, including almost 84,000 alternative schools.

Mid-day Meal Scheme

Of the estimated 205 million child population in the age group 6–14 years on March 1, 2002, nearly 82.5 per cent were enrolled in schools. However, the drop-out rate in 2002-03 was 34.9 per cent at the primary level and 52.8 per cent at the upper primary level. The high drop-out rate has been a matter of major concern. One of the most popular schemes adopted to attract children to schools is the *Mid-day Meal Scheme,* launched in 1995. Several other special programmes have also been launched with varying degrees of success.

Non-governmental Efforts

The bulk of Indian illiterates live in the country's rural areas, where social and economic barriers play an important role in keeping the lowest strata of society illiterate. Government programmes alone, however well intentioned, may not be able to dismantle barriers built over centuries. Major social reformation efforts are sometimes required to bring about a change in the rural scenario.

Asha for Education

Sandeep Pandey won a *Ramon Magsaysay Award* in 2002 in recognition of *"the empowering example of his commitment to the transformation of India's marginalized poor."* While pursuing a *Ph.D.* at the *University of California, Berkeley,* he co-founded *Asha for Education* to support education for poor children in India by tapping the resources of *Overseas Indians,* raising ten thousand dollars in the first year. The organization has since expanded to 36 North-American chapters and disbursed nearly one million dollars for programmes in India.

Pandey has returned to India and works full-time towards Asha's stated mission of bringing about socio-economic change in India through education. Asha's teachers are unpaid volunteers and support themselves with side-occupations, such as making candles and greeting cards from handmade paper. While working with impoverished *low caste* families and *dalits* in *Ballia district* of Uttar Pradesh, Pandey discovered that few children went to school and those that did remained unemployed. With local volunteers, Pandey established schools in the villages of Reoti and Bhainsaha focused on instilling self-reliance and the value of social justice among students. He has also established an *Asha Ashram* in the predominantly Dalit village of Lalpur, outside Lucknow, where students live and study among traditional artisans, and learns the crafts of bee-keeping, vegetable gardening and cottage industries.

Mamidipudi Venkatarangaiya Foundation

Shantha Sinha won a Magsaysay Award in 2003 in recognition of *"her guiding the people of Andhra Pradesh to end the scourge of child labour and send all of their children to school."* As head of an extension programme at the *University of Hyderabad* in 1987, she organized a three-month-long camp to prepare children rescued from *bonded labour* to attend school. Later, in 1991, she guided her family's *Mamidipudi Venkatarangaiya Foundation* to take up this idea as part of its overriding mission in Andhra Pradesh. Her original transition camps grew into full-fledged residential "bridge schools." The foundation's aim is to create a social climate hostile to child labour, *child marriage* and other practices that deny children the right to a normal childhood. Today the MV Foundation's bridge schools and programmes extend to 4,300 villages.

Definition of Literacy

The *United Nations Educational, Scientific and Cultural Organization* (UNESCO) has drafted a definition of literacy as the "ability to identify, understand, interpret, create, communicate, compute and use printed and written materials associated with varying contexts. Literacy involves a continuum of learning in enabling individuals to achieve their goals, to develop their knowledge and potential, and to participate fully in their community and wider society."

The *National Literacy Mission* defines literacy as acquiring the skills of reading, writing and arithmetic and the ability to apply them to one's day-to-day life. The achievement of functional literacy implies (*i*) self-reliance in 3 R's; (*ii*) awareness of the causes of deprivation and the ability to move towards amelioration of their condition by participating in the process of development; (*iii*) acquiring skills to improve economic status and general well being; and (*iv*) imbibing values such as national integration, conservation of environment, women's equality, observance of small family norms.

The working definition of literacy in the Indian *census* since 1991 is as follows:

- ***Literacy rate:*** The total percentage of the population of an area at a particular time aged seven years or above who can read and write with understanding. Here the denominator is the population aged seven years or more.
- ***Crude literacy rate:*** The total percentage of the people of an area at a particular time aged seven years or above who can read and write with understanding, taking the total population of the area (including below seven years of age) as the denominator.

The History of HIV/AIDS in India

At the beginning of 1986, despite over 20,000 reported AIDS cases worldwide, India had no reported cases of HIV or AIDS. There was recognition, though, that this would not be the case for long, and concerns were raised about how India would cope once HIV and AIDS cases started to emerge. One report, published in a medical journal in January 1986, stated: "Unlike developed countries, India lacks the scientific laboratories, research facilities, equipment, and medical personnel to deal with an AIDS epidemic. In addition, factors such as cultural taboos against discussion of sexual practices, poor coordination between local health authorities and their communities, widespread poverty and malnutrition, and a lack of capacity to test and store blood would severely hinder the ability of the Government to control AIDS if the disease did become widespread."

Later in the year, India's first cases of HIV were diagnosed among *sex workers* in Chennai, Tamil Nadu. It was noted that contact with foreign visitors had played a role in initial infections among sex workers, and as HIV screening centres were set up across the country there were calls for visitors to be screened for HIV. Gradually, these calls subsided as more attention was paid to ensuring that HIV screening was carried out in blood banks. In 1987 a National AIDS Control Programme was launched to co-ordinate national responses. Its activities covered surveillance, blood screening, and health education. By the end of 1987, out of 52,907 who had been tested, around 135 people were found to be HIV positive and 14 had AIDS. Most of these initial cases had occurred through heterosexual *sex*, but at the end of the 1980s a rapid spread of HIV was observed among *injecting drug users* (IDUs) in Manipur, Mizoram and Nagaland—three north-eastern states of India bordering Myanmar (Burma).

At the beginning of the 1990s, as infection rates continued to rise, responses were strengthened. In 1992 the government set-up NACO (the National AIDS Control Organisation), to oversee the formulation of policies, prevention work and control programmes relating to HIV and AIDS. In the same year, the government launched a Strategic Plan for HIV prevention. This plan established the administrative and technical basis for programme management and also set-up State AIDS bodies in 25 states and 7 union territories. It was able to make a number of important improvements in HIV prevention such as improving blood safety.

By this stage, cases of HIV infection had been reported in every state of the country. Throughout the 1990s, it was clear that although individual states and cities had separate epidemics, HIV had spread to the general population. Increasingly, cases of infection were observed among people that had previously been seen as *'low-risk'*, such as housewives and richer members of society. In 1998, one author wrote: "HIV infection is now common in India; exactly what the prevalence is, is not really known, but it can be stated without any fear of being wrong that infection is widespread… it is spreading rapidly into those segments that society in India does not recognise as being at risk. AIDS is coming out of the closet."

In 2001, the government adopted the National AIDS Prevention and Control Policy. During that year, former Prime Minister Atal Bihari Vajpayee addressed parliament and referred to HIV/AIDS as one of the most serious health challenges facing the country. Vajpayee also met the chief ministers of the six high-prevalence states to plan the implementation of strategies for HIV/AIDS prevention HIV had now spread extensively throughout the country. In 1990 there had been tens of thousands of people living with HIV in India; by 2000 this had risen to millions.

Current Estimates

In 2006 UNAIDS estimated that there were 5.6 million people living with HIV in India, which indicated that there were more people with HIV in India than in any other country in the world. In 2007, following the first survey of HIV among the general population, UNAIDS and NACO agreed on a new estimate—between 2 million and 3.1 million people living with HIV.

In 2008 the figure was confirmed to be 2.31 million,[19] which equates to a prevalence of 0.3 per cent. While this may seem a low rate, because India's population is so large, it is third in the world in terms of greatest number of people living with HIV. With a population of around a billion, a mere 0.1 per cent increase in HIV prevalence would increase the estimated number of people living with HIV by over half a million. The national HIV prevalence rose dramatically in the early years of the epidemic, but a study released at the beginning of 2006 suggests that the HIV infection rate has recently fallen in southern India, the region that has been hit hardest by AIDS. In addition, NACO released figures in 2008 suggesting that the number of people living with HIV has declined from 2.73 million in 2002 to 2.31 million 2007.

Some AIDS activists are doubtful that the situation is improving:

> "It is the reverse. All the NGOs I know have recorded increases in the number of people accepting help because of HIV. I am really worried that we are just burying our head in the sand over this." *Anjali Gopalan, the Naz Foundation, Delhi* "the statement that India has the AIDS problem under control is not true. There is a decline in prevalence in some of the Southern states... In the rest of the county, there are no arguments to demonstrate that AIDS is under control".

The HIV/AIDS Situation in Different States

The vast size of India makes it difficult to examine the effects of HIV on the country as a whole. The majority of states within India have a higher population than most African countries, so a more detailed picture of the crisis can be gained by looking at each state individually.

The HIV prevalence data for most states is established through testing pregnant women at antenatal clinics. While this means that the data are only directly relevant to sexually active women, they still provide a reasonable indication as to the overall HIV prevalence of each area. The following states have recorded the highest levels of HIV prevalence at antenatal and sexually transmitted disease (STD) clinics over recent years.

Andhra Pradesh

Andhra Pradesh in the southeast of the country has a total population of around 76 million, of whom 6 million live in or around the city of Hyderabad. The HIV prevalence at antenatal clinics was 1 per cent in 2007. This figure is smaller than the reported 1.26 per cent in 2006, but is still highest out of all states. HIV prevalence at STD clinics was very high at 17 per cent in 2007. Among high-risk groups, HIV prevalence was highest among *men who have sex with men* (MSM) (17%), followed by female sex workers (9.7%) and IDUs (3.7%).

Goa

Goa, a popular tourist destination, is a very small state in the southwest of India (population 1.4 million). In 2007 HIV prevalence among antenatal and STD clinic attendees was 0.18 per cent and 5.6 per cent respectively. The Goa State AIDS Control Society reported that in 2008, a record number of 26,737 people were tested for HIV, of which 1018 (3.81%) tested positive.

Karnataka

Karnataka, a diverse state in the southwest of India, has a population of around 53 million. HIV prevalence among antenatal clinic attendees exceeded 1 per cent from 2003 to 2006, and dropped to 0.5 per cent in 2007. Districts with the highest prevalence tend to be located in and around Bangalore in the southern part of the state, or in northern Karnataka's "devadasi belt". Devadasi women are a group of women who have historically been dedicated to the service of gods. These days, this has evolved into sanctioned prostitution, and as a result many women from this part of the country are supplied to the sex trade in big cities such as Mumbai. The average HIV prevalence among female sex workers in Karnataka was just over 5 per cent in 2007, and 17.6 per cent of men who have sex with men were found to be infected.

Maharashtra

Maharashtra is a very large state of three hundred thousand square kilometers, with a total population of around 97 million. The capital city of Maharashtra - Mumbai (Bombay) – is the most populous city in India, with around 14 million inhabitants. The HIV prevalence at antenatal clinics in Maharashtra was 0.5 per cent in 2007. At 18 per cent, the state has the highest reported rates of HIV prevalence among female sex workers. Similarly high rates were found among injecting drug users (24%) and men who have sex with men (12%).

Tamil Nadu

With a population of over 66 million, Tamil Nadu is the seventh most populous state in India. Between 1995 and 1997 HIV prevalence among pregnant women tripled to around 1.25 per cent. The State Government subsequently set up an AIDS society, which aimed to focus on HIV prevention initiatives. A safe-sex campaign was launched, encouraging *condom* use and attacking the stigma and ignorance associated with HIV. Between 1996 and 1998 a survey showed that the number of men reporting high-risk sexual behaviour had decreased. In 2007 HIV prevalence among antenatal clinic attendees was 0.25 per cent. HIV prevalence among injecting drug users was 16.8%, third highest out of all reporting states. HIV prevalence among men who have sex with men and female sex workers was 6.6 per cent and 4.68 per cent respectively.

Manipur

Manipur is a small state of some 2.4 million people in northeast India. Manipur borders Myanmar (Burma), one of the world's largest producers of illicit opium. In the early 1980s drug use became popular in northeast India and it wasn't long before

HIV was reported among injecting drug users in the region. Although NACO report a state-wise HIV prevalence of 17.9 per cent among IDUs, studies from different areas of the state find prevalence to be as high as 32 per cent. HIV is no longer confined to IDUs, but has spread further to the general population. HIV prevalence at antenatal clinics in Manipur exceeded 1 per cent in recent years, but then declined to 0.75 per cent in 2007. Estimated adult HIV prevalence is the highest out of all states, at 1.57 per cent.

Mizoram

The small northeastern state of Mizoram has fewer than a million inhabitants. In 1998, an HIV epidemic took off quickly among the state's male injecting drug users, with some drug clinics registering HIV rates of more than 70 per cent among their patients. In recent years the average prevalence among this group has been much lower, at around 3-7 per cent. HIV prevalence at antenatal clinics was 0.75 per cent in 2007.

Nagaland

Nagaland is another small northeastern state where injecting drug use has again been the driving force behind the spread of HIV. In 2003 HIV prevalence among IDUs was 8.43 per cent, but has since declined to 1.91 per cent in 2007. HIV prevalence at antenatal clinics and STD clinics was 0.60 per cent and 3.42 per cent respectively in 2007.

The Punjab

The Punjab, a state in northern mainland India, has shown an increase in prevalence among injecting drug users (13.8% in 2007) in recent years. One of the richest cities in the Punjab, Ludhiana, has an HIV prevalence of 21 per cent among IDUs. Denis Broun, head of UNAIDS in India has stated..."the problem of IDUs has been underestimated in mainland India, as most of the problem was thought to be in the northeast."

Who is Affected by HIV and AIDS in India?

People living with HIV in India come from incredibly diverse cultures and backgrounds. The vast majority of infections occur through heterosexual sex (80%), and most of those who become infected would not fall into the category of 'high-risk groups'—although members of such groups, including sex workers, men who have sex with men, truck drivers and migrant workers, do face a disproportionately higher risk of infection. See Table 6.2 page 103 on *affected groups in India* for more information.

HIV Prevention

Educating people about HIV/AIDS and how it can be prevented is complicated in India, as a number of major languages and hundreds of different dialects are spoken within its population. This means that, although some *HIV/AIDS prevention* and education can be done at the national level, many of the efforts are best carried out at the state and local level.

Each state has its own AIDS Prevention and Control Society, which carries out local initiatives with guidance from NACO. Under the second stage of the government's National AIDS Control Programme (NACP-II), which finished in March 2006, state AIDS control societies were granted funding for youth campaigns, blood safety checks, and HIV testing, among other things. Various public platforms were used to raise awareness of the epidemic—concerts, radio dramas, a voluntary blood donation day and TV spots with a popular Indian film-star. Messages were also conveyed to young people through schools. Teachers and peer educators were trained to teach about the subject, and students were educated through active learning sessions, including debates and role-play.

The third stage of the National AIDS Control Programme (NACP-III), was launched in July 2007 and runs until 2012. The programme has a budget of around $2.6 billion, two thirds of which is for prevention and one sixth for treatment. Aside from the government, this money will come from non-governmental organisations, companies, and international agencies, such as the World Bank and the Bill and Melinda Gates Foundation. The government has announced that this campaign will place a strong focus on condom promotion. It has already supported the installation of over 11,000 condom vending machines in colleges, road-side restaurants, stations, gas stations and hospitals. With support from the United States Agency for International Development (USAID), the government has also initiated a campaign called 'Condom Bindas Bol!' (Condom-Just say it!), which involves advertising, public events and celebrity endorsements. It aims to break the taboo that currently surrounds condom use in India, and to persuade people that they should not be embarrassed to buy them.

In one unique scheme, health activists in West Bengal are attempting to promote condom use through kite flying, which is popular before the state's biggest festival, Durga Puja: "The colourful kites carry the message that using a condom is a simple and instinctive act… they can fly high in the sky and land at distant places where we cannot reach." This initiative is an example of how HIV prevention campaigns in India can be tailored to the situations of different states and areas. In doing so, they can make an important impact, particularly in rural areas where information is often lacking. Small-scale campaigns like this are often run or supported by non-governmental organisations, which play a vital role in preventing infections throughout India, particularly among high-risk groups. In some cases, members of these risk groups have formed their own organisations to respond to the epidemic.

The government has however funded a small number of national campaigns to spread awareness about HIV/AIDS to complement the local level initiatives. On World AIDS Day 2007 India flagged off its largest national campaign to date, in the form of a seven-coach train called the 'Red Ribbon Express.' A year later the train journey was completed, having travelled to 180 stations in 24 states and reaching around 6.2 million people with HIV/AIDS education and awareness.

PMTCT

In 2004 only 5 per cent of pregnant women living with HIV received antiretroviral to prevent mother-to-child transmission. By 2007 this had risen to 14 per cent but with such low coverage 21,000 children below the age of 15 are still infected every year through mother-to-child transmission in India.

Testing

The general consensus among those fighting AIDS worldwide is that *HIV testing* should be carried out voluntarily, with the consent of the individual concerned. This view has been supported by the Indian government and NACO, who have helped to establish hundreds of integrated counselling and testing centres (ICTCs) in India. By the end of 2008 there were 4817 ICTCs in India, compared to just 62 in 1997. In 2007 these centres tested 5.9 million people for HIV, an increase from 0.14 million in 2001.

Although voluntary testing is officially supported in India, some states have tried to implement policies that would force people to be tested for HIV against their will. In Goa and Andhra Pradesh the state governments proposed a bill in 2006 to make HIV tests compulsory before marriage, and in Punjab it has been proposed that all people wishing to obtain or retain a driver's license should be tested for HIV. Neither of these plans has come to pass, but they have concerned activists, who argue that HIV testing should never be imposed on people against their wishes.

Unfortunately, cases of people being tested without their consent or knowledge are common in Indian hospitals. In one 2002 study, it was suggested that over 95 per cent of patients listed for surgical procedures are tested against their will, often resulting in their surgery being cancelled. Hospital staff and health professionals, much like the rest of the Indian population, are often unaware of the facts about HIV. This leads to unnecessary fears and, in some cases, causes them to stigmatise HIV positive people and discriminate against them, including testing them without consent. India has certainly made progress in expanding HIV testing to its large population. However, considering only 50 per cent of those currently infected with HIV are aware of their status there is still significant work to be done in this area.

Treatment for People Living with HIV

Antiretroviral drugs (ARVs), which can significantly delay the progression from HIV to AIDS—have been available in developed countries since 1996. Unfortunately, as in many resource-poor areas, access to this treatment is limited in India; an estimated 285,000 people were receiving ARVs by November 2009 through government health centres and another 35,000 through private health facilities. This represents less than half of those estimated to be in need of antiretroviral treatment in India.

While the coverage of treatment remains unacceptably low, improvements are being made. The government has started to expand access to ARVs in a number of areas; by November 2009 there were 266 reported sites providing antiretroviral therapy. Increasing access to ARVs also means that an increasing number of people living with HIV in India are developing drug resistance. When HIV becomes resistant to the ARVs the treatment regimen needs to be changed to 'second-line' ARVs. As with many other parts of the world, second-line treatment in India is far more expensive than first-line treatment.

In 2008, NACO began to roll out government funded second-line antiretroviral treatment in two centres in Mumbai and Chennai. By 2009 second-line therapy was available in a total of eight states but treatment remains very limited. Of the 3,000 who need to be on second line treatment, about 750 were receiving it as of December 2009. One reason for this is expense; second line ARV drugs, unlike first line ARVs, are not produced on a large scale in India due to patent issues that control *drug pricing* and can be more than 10 times more expensive than first line ARVs. Another reason why coverage is so limited is the eligibility requirements imposed on second line ARVs; only those 'living below the poverty line, widows and children' and those who have received first-line ARVs from a government centre for at least two years are eligible.

Ironically, India is a major provider of cheap generic copies of ARVs to countries all over the world. However, the large scale of India's epidemic, the diversity of its spread, and the country's lack of finances and resources continue to present barriers to India's antiretroviral treatment programme. "It is a sad irony that India is one of the biggest producers of the drugs that have transformed the lives of people with AIDS in wealthy countries. But for millions of Indians, access to these medicines is a distant dream" *Joanne Csete, Director of the HIV/ AIDS programme at Human Rights Watch.*

Stigma and Discrimination in India

In India, as elsewhere, AIDS is often seen as *"someone else's problem"*—as something that affects people living on the margins of society, whose lifestyles are considered immoral. Even as it moves into the general population, the HIV epidemic is still misunderstood among the Indian public. People living with HIV have faced violent attacks, been rejected by families, spouses and communities, been refused medical treatment, and even, in some reported cases, denied the last rites before they die. As well as adding to the suffering of people living with HIV, this discrimination is hindering efforts to prevent new infections. While such strong reactions to HIV and AIDS exist, it is difficult to educate people about how they can avoid infection. AIDS outreach workers and peer-educators have reported harassment, and in schools, teachers sometimes face negative reactions from the parents of children that they teach about AIDS: "When I discussed with my mother about having an AIDS education programme, she said, 'you learn and come home and talk about it in the neighbourhood, they will kick you'. She feels that we should not talk about it."

Discrimination is also alarmingly common in the health care sector. Negative attitudes from health care staff have generated anxiety and fear among many people living with HIV and AIDS. As a result, many keep their status secret. It is not surprising that for many HIV positive people, AIDS-related fear and anxiety, and at times denial of their HIV status, can be traced to traumatic experiences in health care settings. "There is an almost hysterical kind of fear ... at all levels, starting from the humblest, the sweeper or the ward boy, up to the heads of departments, which make them pathologically scared of having to deal with an HIV positive patient. Wherever they have an HIV patient, the responses are shameful."

A 2006 study found that 25 per cent of people living with HIV in India had been refused medical treatment on the basis of their HIV-positive status. It also found strong evidence of stigma in the workplace, with 74 per cent of employees not disclosing their status to their employees for fear of discrimination. Of the 26 per cent who did disclose their status, 10 per cent reported having faced prejudice as a result. People in marginalized groups—female sex workers, hijras (transgender) and *gay* men—are often stigmatised not only because of their HIV status, but also because they belong to socially excluded groups.

Stigma is made worse by a lack of knowledge about AIDS. Although a high percentage of people have heard about HIV and AIDS in urban areas (94% of men and 83% of women) this is much lower in rural areas where only 77 per cent of men and 50 per cent of women have heard of HIV and AIDS. However, the real challenge lies with ignorance about how

HIV is transmitted—for example the majority of men and women in rural areas believe that AIDS can be transmitted by mosquito bites. In 2009, NACO carried a population based survey in Nagaland, which showed that 72.8 per cent of people believed HIV could be transmitted by sharing food with someone.

The Future of HIV and AIDS in India

Various groups have made predictions about the effect that AIDS will have on India and the rest of *Asia* in the future, and there has been a lot of dispute about the accuracy of these estimates. For instance, a 2002 report by the CIA's National Intelligence Council predicted 20 million to 25 million AIDS cases in India by 2010—more than any other country in the world. India's government responded by calling these figures completely inaccurate, and accused those who cited them of spreading panic. The government has also disputed predictions that India's epidemic is on an African trajectory, although it claims to acknowledge the seriousness of the crisis.

Indeed, recent surveys do suggest that national HIV prevalence has probably fallen slightly in recent years. This trend is mainly due to a drop in infections in southern states; in other areas there has been no significant decline. "In the north-east, the dual HIV epidemic driven by unsafe sex and injecting drug use is highly concerning. Moreover, there are many areas in the northern states where HIV is increasing, particularly among injecting drug users." *Sujatha Rao, Director General of NACO.*

HIV spending has been steadily increasing in India in recent years. In 2006-2007 $171 million was spent to contain and prevent the growth of HIV, which represented an increase of 28 per cent from the previous year. Currently, India spends about 5 per cent of its health budget on HIV and AIDS. However, the World Bank has warned that India will have to scale up prevention efforts in order to avoid spending more of its health budget in the future. According to the World

Bank's report, by 2020 India will have to spend 7 per cent of its health budget on AIDS if the rising tide of the AIDS epidemic in New Delhi, Mumbai, the north and the north east is not halted. This would put further strain on a struggling health sector which, on top of HIV and AIDS, faces a growing multitude of health challenges including malaria, diabetes, heart disease and cancer.

Even if the country's epidemic does not match the severity of those in southern Africa, it is clear that HIV and AIDS will have a devastating effect on the lives of millions of Indians for many years to come. It is essential that effective action is taken to minimize this impact.

Table 6.2 : Specimen Data Tables : Demographics

Statewise (Census 2001) State	Population in India				
	Total	Male	%	Female	%
INDIA	1027015247	531277078	51.7	495738169	48.3
Jammu & Kashmir	10069917	5300574	52.6	4769343	47.4
Himachal Pradesh	6077248	3085256	50.8	2991992	49.2
Punjab	24289296	12963362	53.4	11325934	46.6
Chandigarh	900914	508224	56.4	392690	43.6
Uttaranchal	8479562	4316401	50.9	4163161	49.1
Haryana	21082989	11327658	53.7	9755331	46.3
Delhi	13782976	7570890	54.9	6212086	45.1
Rajasthan	56473122	29381657	52	27091465	48
Uttar Pradesh	166052859	87466301	52.7	78586558	47.3
Bihar	82878796	43153964	52.1	39724832	47.9
Sikkim	540493	288217	53.3	252276	46.7
Arunachal Pradesh	1091117	573951	52.6	517166	47.4
Nagaland	1988636	1041686	52.4	946950	47.6
Manipur	2388634	1207338	50.5	1181296	49.5
Mizoram	891058	459783	51.6	431275	48.4

Statewise (Census 2001) State	Population in India				
	Total	Male	%	Female	%
Tripura	3191168	1636138	51.3	1555030	48.7
Meghalaya	2306069	1167840	50.6	1138229	49.4
Assam	26638407	13787799	51.8	12850608	48.2
West Bengal	80221171	41487694	51.7	38733477	48.3
Jharkhand	26909428	13861277	51.5	13048151	48.5
Orissa	36706920	18612340	50.7	18094580	49.3
Chhatisgarh	20795956	10452426	50.3	10343530	49.7
Madhya Pradesh	60385118	31456873	52.1	28928245	47.9
Gujarat	50596992	26344053	52.1	24252939	47.9
Daman & Diu	158059	92478	58.5	65581	41.5
Dadra & Nagar Haveli	220451	121731	55.2	98720	44.8
Maharashtra	96752247	50334270	52	46417977	48
Andhra Pradesh	75727541	38286811	50.6	37440730	49.4
Karnataka	52733958	26856343	50.9	25877615	49.1
Goa	1343998	685617	51	658381	49
Lakshadweep	60595	31118	51.4	29477	48.6
Kerala	31838619	15468664	48.6	16369955	51.4
Tamil Nadu	62110839	31268654	50.3	30842185	49.7
Pondicherry	973829	486705	50	487124	50
Andaman & Nicobar Islands	356265	192985	54.2	163280	45.8

Per cent Distribution of Estimated Population by Age-group, Sex and Residence in India (1999)

Age-Group	Total			Rural			Urban		
	Total	Male	Female	Total	Male	Female	Total	Male	Female
0-4	11.6	11.8	11.5	12.2	12.4	12.0	10.0	10.1	9.9
5-9	11.2	11.3	11.1	11.7	11.8	11.6	9.9	9.9	9.8
10-14	12.0	12.2	11.8	12.3	12.5	12.0	11.0	11.1	10.9
15-19	10.3	10.6	9.9	10.2	10.6	9.8	10.3	10.4	10.2
20-24	9.2	9.1	9.3	8.8	8.8	8.9	10.1	9.9	10.4
25-29	8.1	8.0	8.2	7.9	7.7	8.0	8.9	8.9	8.9
30-34	7.5	7.3	7.8	7.3	7.0	7.6	8.2	8.1	8.2

Age-Group	Total			Rural			Urban		
	Total	Male	Female	Total	Male	Female	Total	Male	Female
35-39	6.3	6.3	6.4	6.1	6.1	6.2	6.9	6.9	6.9
40-44	5.7	5.7	5.7	5.5	5.5	5.5	6.3	6.3	6.3
45-49	4.4	4.5	4.3	4.2	4.3	4.2	4.9	5.2	4.6
50-54	3.8	3.8	3.8	3.7	3.7	3.8	4.0	4.1	3.9
55-59	2.9	2.9	2.9	2.8	2.8	2.9	2.9	3.0	2.8
60-64	2.5	2.4	2.7	2.6	2.4	2.7	2.3	2.2	2.4
65-69	2.0	1.9	2.1	2.0	1.9	2.1	1.8	1.7	1.9
70-74	1.3	1.2	1.4	1.3	1.2	1.4	1.2	1.1	1.3
75-79	0.7	0.7	0.8	0.7	0.7	0.8	0.7	0.6	0.7
80-84	0.3	0.3	0.4	0.3	0.3	0.4	0.3	0.3	0.3
85+	0.2	0.2	0.2	0.2	0.2	0.2	0.2	0.2	0.2
Total	**100.0**	**100.0**	**100.0**	**100.0**	**100.0**	**100.0**	**100.0**	**100.0**	**100.0**

Growth of Indian Population by Sex (1901-11 to 1991-2001)

Year	Average Annual Exponential Growth rate Per cent		
	Female	Male	Total
1901-1911	0.53	0.61	0.56
1911-1921	-0.08	0.01	-0.03
1921-1931	1.01	1.06	1.04
1931-1941	1.30	1.36	1.33
1941-1951	1.27	1.25	1.25
1951-1961	1.93	1.99	1.96
1961-1971	2.15	2.27	2.22
1971-1981*	2.23	2.13	2.20
1981-1991**	2.10	2.17	2.14
1991-2001	1.97	1.90	1.94

Note: * The 1981 Census could not be held in Assam. The Population figures for 1981 for Assam worked out by interpolation have been included.

** The 1991 Census was not held in Jammu & Kashmir. The population figures include projected population of Jammu & Kashmir as projected by the Standing Committee of Experts on population projections (Oct 1989).

Data table headings are shown Year-wise in descending order)

Summary-Training and Employment Opportunities

Several organizations in three countries, including NYC in the Philippines, DoVE and DSD in Thailand, and MARD in Viet Nam, have undertaken measures to provide training for the rural youth. However, there was limited access to formal training in all the survey sites. This was either because such training programmes did not exist, or the respondents were unaware of them. While a few respondents in each surveyed sites had informal training from their parents, almost all respondents expressed an interest in receiving formal training.

In terms of employment, an evident trend is the influx of rural youth into the urban areas in search of employment. This is against the backdrop of the concentration of employment opportunities in urban areas, especially those created due to trade and technology advancements in the manufacturing and service sectors. Meanwhile, the field studies suggested potential for community-based employment opportunities. The areas of employment common to the three countries are tourism, handicraft making (such as bamboo, rattan crafts and embroidery), and service related work (such as motorcycle delivery, security guard and domestic work), in addition to fishing (in the case of the Philippines), and agribusiness and construction (in the case of Thailand), and brick making and infrastructure projects, and public sector works, including teaching and commune office work (in the case of Viet Nam).

Recommendations

Policy Co-ordination

The findings from the country studies demonstrated that there are four, interrelated areas of major challenges with regard to employment and training of the rural youth. These areas are education, training, employment and income generation, and labour market information. While the governments of the Philippines, Thailand and Viet Nam have all sought to address concerns in these areas, local level impacts have been limited. This is due to the limited human (both in number and quality) and financial resources particularly in terms of reaching the local and community levels.

Recommendation (1): There is a need for better policy co-ordination, both among national level government agencies and between the national and local level government agencies, as a means to address the challenges relating to resource limitations including their use and effective policy implementation. In addition, decentralization of implementation may also be pursued, on the condition that appropriate monitoring and evaluation are provided by the respective central and/or decentralized governments. It is also essential to ensure broad-based ownership in improving the employment and training prospects of the rural youth, through capacity building of the staff involved, as well as collaboration with other stakeholders, such as labour market institutions (*i.e.,* employers' and workers' organizations, and representatives of interest groups, such as youth associations).

This section summarizes the opportunities and challenges concerning the promotion of training and employment among the rural youth, and presents recommendations.

Employment and Income Generation

Rather than a lack of employment opportunities *per se,* a major issue is a lack of decent work opportunities. While large numbers of rural youth migrate to urban areas, they are often disappointed by a lack of such opportunities. The youth may prefer to stay in rural areas provided that employment and income generation opportunities are improved.

Recommendation (2a): Given the important role of agriculture in rural communities, priority must be directed towards improving productivity in the agricultural sector, which can contribute to economic development and poverty reduction in rural areas. Livelihood diversification, along with the application of improved agri-business and technology application, can be explored.

Recommendation (2b): It is critical to create options for the rural youth to seek employment in rural areas through creating and improving the quality of employment in the on, off and non-farm sectors. In this undertaking, it is important to take local contexts into account to ensure that knowledge and skills attained are in line with rural labour markets and employment needs.

Recommendation (2c): There is a need to promote an entrepreneurial culture and enabling environment for youth in wage- and/or self-employment sectors. Entrepreneurship provides greater opportunities for employment, skills development, as well as innovation in products and services. Consideration needs to be taken that entrepreneurship does not come at the expense of education.

Recommendation (2d): It is important to place greater emphasis on improving access to micro-credit schemes, financial/business training, business development services and market information, as a means to encourage youth entrepreneurial activity/self employment.

Training

In addition to the availability and affordability of training, a major issue facing the rural youth is the lack of information and resultant awareness among the youth, their families and communities on the available training, particularly the ones meeting labour market demands. In addition, the youth or their families do not deem the time spent in training as a desirable trade-off to earning immediate income which may come from a low-paying and low-productivity job.

Recommendation (3a): In order to ensure the quality and relevance of training, efforts must be made to first assess the labour market needs in the given local context, and then to create opportunities for skills training to meet these needs, as well as the preferences of the rural youth.

Recommendation (3b): It is important to encourage families and the rural youth to recognize the benefits of training, while disseminating information on available training opportunities, scholarships, youth programmes, and job fairs through the use of appropriate media, such as newspapers, television and radio. The promotion of training should not come at the expense of higher level education, but can be promoted in such a way as to supplement formal education.

Recommendation (3c): It is important to secure funding for training programmes to benefit the current and future youth, and make training affordable and accessible to women and disadvantaged groups.

Formal Education

The main barriers to formal education identified from the case studies are access, affordability, quality and relevance, particularly in rural areas where physical access to secondary schools is difficult and the incidence of poverty is high. An added problem is a lack of teachers, appropriate learning equipment and infrastructure.

Recommendation (4a): Countries should continue to strive for free, quality education and training up until the minimum working age. For those countries still striving to achieve free basic education, lowering the direct (*e.g.*, school fees) and indirect costs (*e.g.*, text books, uniforms, transport) of education can help prevent early school drop-out among poor families and ensure that young people have a smooth transition from school to work in the rural and remote areas.

Recommendation (4b): There is a need for continuous efforts to ensure gender parity and raise overall equality in education for migrant, minority, working children, and otherwise marginalized, disadvantaged groups in order for inclusive and easily accessible education.

Recommendation (4c): In order to improve the quality of education available for rural youth, greater investment is needed to ensure adequate classroom materials, safe and well-maintained school environments, quality of teachers through training, along with better remuneration.

Labour Market Information

There is a scarcity of labour market information in general, particularly in rural areas. This is an obstacle for governments to devise informed policies and also for the youth to make informed decisions on employment and training. It is also a challenge in matching the supply and needs of rural youth with the demands of the labour market.

Recommendation (5a): It is essential to strengthen the promotion and dissemination of information on the opportunities and services that are available to rural youth, as well as the risks and benefits associated with migration to urban areas or abroad. Appropriate media needs to be used, such as radio, newspapers, television, internet and leaflets, in addition to schools and training institutions, as well as call centres and private companies.

Recommendation (5b): It is important to enhance employment assistance and career guidance for rural youths by creating and improving facilities in rural areas with trained professionals and access to technologies such as Internet-based information databases.

Country Specific Observations and Recommendations

The following country specific observations are highlighted as possible areas for country specific recommendations and follow up action:

Philippines

- "Ladderized education", (*i.e.*, the breaking-up of the four-year curricular programme into several associate programmes that can be completed in one or two years) can be explored. Upon the completion of one associate programme, students can either seek employment or pursue the next level associate programme until a Baccalaureate degree is obtained.

- Emphasis should be placed on creating jobs in the areas of business and entrepreneurship, ICTs, tourism related services and environment and sustainable development related occupations. There is also the need to focus more on ICT employment opportunities in rural areas, such as call centres, business procurement outsourcing, and internet cafes. The youth are generally knowledgeable about ICT, and are well placed to take advantage of such job opportunities. ICTs are also a source for labour market information.
- Institutions such as the National Youth Commission and the Technical Education and Skills Development Authority, as well as local NGOs are well placed to disseminate information regarding grants, and scholarships available to youth, and the labour market.

Thailand

- His Majesty the King's philosophy of a "sufficiency economy", which stresses balanced development and highlights the importance of development of each a region relevant to their resource conditions, is considered essential to the development and integration of the principles of the sufficiency economy into the school curriculum. This concept should be further encouraged and strengthened. The principles and farm-level diversification should be further explored to reduce unemployment among the rural poor. Educational opportunities for youth in remote and poor areas should be broader, more diverse and more flexible to meet diver se backgrounds, needs and abilities. In addition, strategies should be developed to promote co-operative enterprises and social services, as well as an entrepreneurial culture. These initiatives are an important means of enhancing job opportunities for the rural youth.

Viet Nam

- It is particularly important in Viet Nam to create community-based employment opportunities, since the country study indicated that many youths would prefer to stay in rural areas provided that better training, employment and income generation opportunities are available. In this regard, areas of off-farm employment to be explored include bamboo and rattan product and handicraft making. These can supply marketable and environmentally friendly products while providing income generation opportunities for the youth.
- The export of labour to other countries is a priority in Viet Nam's employment strategy. This may be pursued as a means to develop the technical skills of the rural youth who, upon returning to their country, could contribute to a raised human resource capacity. This programme needs to be balanced with appropriate and sustained investment in enhancing co-ordinated education, training and decent work opportunities in rural communities.

Key Publications

- World Youth Reports 2003, 2005 and 2007.
- Guide to the Implementation of the World Programme of Action for Youth.
- Making Commitments Matter: A Toolkit for young people to Evaluate National Youth Policy.
- A Brief Guide to Youth Delegates to the United Nations General Assembly.
- Various Reports of the Secretary-General related to youth issues.

Index

M

N